Green Housekeeping

RECIPES AND SOLUTIONS FOR A CLEANER, MORE SUSTAINABLE HOME

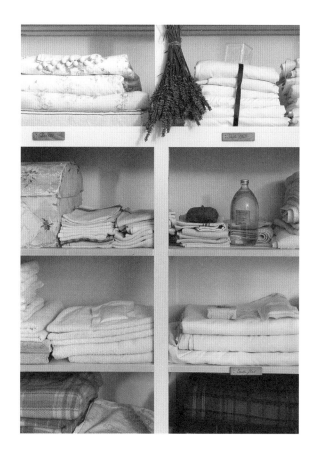

Christina Strutt OF CABBAGES & ROSES

CICO BOOKS

LONDON NEW YORK

This edition published in 2019 by CICO Books
an imprint of Ryland Peters & Small Ltd
20–21 Jockey's Fields   341 E 116th St
London WC1R 4BW   New York, NY 10029

www.rylandpeters.com

10 9 8 7 6 5 4 3 2 1

First published in 2008 as *Cabbages & Roses Guide to Natural Housekeeping* and in 2012 as *A Guide to Natural Housekeeping*

A CIP catalog record for this book is available from the Library of Congress and the British Library.

ISBN: 978 1 78249 783 7

Printed in China

Project editors: Marion Paull and Gillian Haslam
Text editor: Samantha Gray
Designer: Christine Wood
Photographer: Lucinda Symons
Illustrators: Trina Dalziel and Michael Hill

In-house editor: Anna Galkina
Art director: Sally Powell
Head of production: David Hearn
Publishing manager: Penny Craig
Publisher: Cindy Richards

Always consult a doctor or qualified herbalist before treating any ailment. While every attempt has been made to ensure the information in this book is entirely safe, correct and up-to-date at the time of publication, the Publishers accept no responsibility for consequences of the advice given herein. The Publishers also accept no responsibility for changes in stockists and locations mentioned herein.

Green Housekeeping

CONTENTS

INTRODUCTION

When I first wrote this book, my thoughts were of preserving a world for my then-imagined grandchildren. It felt imperative. We had to change the habits of our daily domestic lives to counteract the effects of climate change. A decade later, the effect of living beyond our ecological means has raised the status of this imperative to urgent. We must—each of us— work together for the benefit of our planet if we wish our children, let alone our grandchildren, to enjoy a fraction of the Earth's bounty and beauty we have known.

Today, this book feels even more personal, since those precious grandchildren no longer exist only in the realm of my imagination. Indeed, for every one of us, this battle must be personal if it is to be won. Planet Earth is a resilient place: as humanity's canvas it has absorbed much and made way for so many of our inventions. Mankind is clever—too clever, perhaps. Our species has now entered its sixth millennia on the planet, and it is clear that for all our brilliance, wisdom has proved elusive—or is willfully ignored. We cannot continue to think only of convenience and the immediate future. We need to change our ways to make sure that our beautiful planet can support us for many generations to come.

If this sounds a gloomy premise for a book, it is meant neither to depress nor to despair. In fact, I have come back to this book for precisely the opposite reason: to look for the spring shoots of hope, and for ways in which we can all, without difficulty, effect change. Because there is good news. While scientists now talk openly about having passed the point of no return, they also assure us that if we mean business, we can make a difference. Governments need to respond quickly and decisively—there must be no denial of the facts. But change starts at home and, if we are united, the effect of such change could be dramatic.

The nightly news may seem dismal, but there are chinks of light. I can see that the generation coming of age now really cares. They shall inherit this earth and they have no intention of being meek. I see community projects—the co-operatively kept hens that feed a neighborhood, the community gardens—and I see daily rounds of YouTube videos with ingenious ideas for repurposing the plastic we have consumed. I see the small businesses using compostable materials where plastics were once used, and I see a growing rejection of consumerism. As the owner of a business that sells clothes, you may see a contradiction. Second to oil, the clothing and textile industry is the largest polluter in the world. At present, the market produces too much, and the cheaper clothing is, the less we value it. We are buying four times as many clothes today as we did ten years ago, and we are wearing them for half the amount of time. In 2018 in the UK, we sent £12.5 billion ($16.3 billion) worth of clothing to landfill—equating to 300,000 tons of textiles. On average, each person threw away eight items, meaning that each British household wasted clothes with a value of almost £500 ($650). We all need to buy fewer, better pieces; we do not need to constantly replenish—rather, we need to buy what we love and love what we buy for a long, long time.

Our aim at Cabbages & Roses is to make clothes that last, that will be loved by at least two, if not three generations, that will be mended, patched, passed on, resold or repurposed. We produce "slow" clothes; made in the UK in limited quantities and to last a lifetime. We are striving to reduce our carbon footprint wherever possible, aiming to use organic fabrics, and to know the provenance of everything we use. We are finding ways to avoid chemicals, plastics, and waste. Through these pages, I hope to share home- and community-applicable

SMALL CHANGES, BIG REWARDS

In 1987 the world began living beyond its sustainable means. Our ecological credit card is over its limit and the interest is in overdrive. Just as "every little helps" when climbing out of the financial debt mire, every individual making small changes will start to clear this terrible, world-changing, debt.

"The effect of a billion people working together will not only be a huge political mandate for change—it will also buy us time to develop longterm sustainable solutions to defeat global warming."

Julian Knight, chief executive of Global Cool www.globalcool.org

"We must rediscover our links with the natural environment if we are to tread more lightly on the world."

Craig Simmons, cofounder of Best Foot Forward

methods—big and small—to create less waste and to reuse that which we do buy. And since we're in the second decade of this century, and almost everyone has use of the Internet, I would love the readers of this book to share their own tips via social media. This is a rallying-cry to adopt ideas for sustainable living, many of which tap into ancient ways and our collective consciousness. I hope that this book assists you in making those switches in every aspect of your domestic life.

Let us together do no harm.

This is a guide to changing your entire way of life. Just as important as how to make raspberry cordial, making the most of the fruits that come once a year, is to be aware of the nontoxic solutions you can use to clean up the kitchen afterward. This is not a guide to sacrifice and hardship; on the contrary, it is a guide to embracing the gifts we have with great pleasure.

If, in years to come, it is established that there was nothing we could have done to prevent global warming, the suggestions in this book can do no harm. If, however, in future we see that together we all made a huge difference to climate change and the disasters it might have caused, then we can congratulate ourselves on a job well done. We will be the beneficiaries of a world with a healthy population where fairness is the embodiment of ecological politics, and safety is at the heart of farming and manufacturing.

Preparing your own cleaning products and growing your own organic fruit and vegetables is a safer, more ecologically sound way of living. This guide will hopefully encourage more people to see the damage we are doing to the environment by relying on carbon fuels, chemicals, and fertilizers to sustain our lifestyle. It is possible to keep a clean house and maintain a fertile garden organically, to shop locally and seasonally, and to recycle and reuse as much as we possibly can. This way of life may sometimes be more time consuming but, having tried and tested all the recipes in this book, I have found that it is more efficient and ultimately much simpler and less stressful. Add to that the fact that you will save money, the environment and miles traveled, and this can only be a good thing.

"Poor people are directly dependent on biodiversity and strong ecosystems, and are most vulnerable to their degradation. With out proper valuation, our lofty aspirations for Africa will not be achieved."

Kaveh Zahedi

Life in the twenty-first century

Our lives have changed immeasurably during the past century and life has become so much easier, richer, and more comfortable for those of us lucky enough to be born in the affluent, developed parts of the world.

We have become fatter, lazier, more tired, more stressed and more dependent on mood-altering/enhancing concoctions. We demand instant cures for the ills we find ourselves suffering from, be it antibiotics for a slight cough or outrageously expensive preparations which promise us that they will prevent old age becoming visible on our faces. Our homes can be sparkling clean and germfree with the thousands of cleaning products served to us, as it were, on a nice clean plate. Life has become terribly, terribly easy. This clean and easy way of life is having a huge impact on our lives and environment. It is, quite literally, making us and our world very, very ill.

During the past 100 years scientists, doctors, industrialists, farmers and governments have developed cures for our ailments and solutions to all our needs. Governments and food suppliers—always under pressure to meet the demand for cheap food—have responded with the help of science and air miles. We believed that they knew best and we were grateful for their expert knowledge. In fairness, we have, as they say, never had it so good, but at what cost? It was accepted as good practice to feed brains and spinal cords to herbivores to increase their growth rate, thereby increasing profit and reducing the need for the green fields upon which they would naturally graze. DDT, banned in 1973, was once universally accepted as an effective and safe pesticide. Antibiotics and growth hormones are still routinely given to farm animals. Organically reared livestock survive and thrive without.

"It is evident in the world around us that very dramatic changes are taking place."

Al Gore: An Inconvenient Truth

We have all lived through food scares and epidemics. Largely to blame are murky regulations and badly enforced laws on animal husbandry, poor food safety, manufacturing, and production. There is no universal regime for imported foodstuffs requiring them to demonstrate high standards of animal husbandry or to be labeled with information concerning provenance.

Look back at the lives of our forefathers who worked with nature and had the expertise to be self-sufficient. Living organically and self-sufficiently need not preclude importing from other countries, but it does mean that should the necessity arise, we would be capable of survival without outside help.

We have expended such energy on fighting Mother Nature in the name of progress and protecting ourselves from her tantrums that we forget to feel gratitude for her bounty. The time has come to stop and smell the roses, to take stock of the damage we have done and are doing, and quietly, gently, wisely alter our habits.

> *"You can shove nature out with a pitchfork,*
> *but she'll keep coming back."*
>
> Traditional proverb

There is a great deal that we can do to make the world a better place. We are all aware of the impending disasters awaiting us if we continue on the path we are taking. The time will come, I feel sure, when the extravagance and unconsidered comfort we have grown to expect will become a thing of the past. We are so unaware of how our cheap food is produced it is terribly easy to throw away almost half of what we buy. In order to understand the real value of food, we need to consider our wasteful nature, pay fair rewards to farmers for their labors and support them by shopping locally and seasonally.

Growing one's own fruit and vegetables certainly encourages frugality, deference, and pride. Apart from the immense pleasure it gives, knowing how to grow food is, I feel, something that is becoming increasingly important. It is good to know the cost of food, but better still to know its value.

The most wholesome path to take in preventing the global warming catastrophe before it is too late is to stop accepting the unacceptable. In this book I hope to enlighten you on how to lead life in a more thoughtful, careful, organic, and ecologically friendly way. It is unlikely that many of us have the wherewithal to take on governments or food suppliers. However, it is within the scope of every one of us to vote with our wallet and custom, to protect ourselves and our families, to take charge of every molecule we ingest and every product we buy. As I write, I am aware that big business is investing in the organic revolution, presumably directed by market forces. Consumers are demanding good, honest, natural products from ecologically sensitive and sound, sustainable sources.

Working with nature

The most important and potentially lifesaving gift we can give to our children is to teach them to have respect for, and to be aware of, the life-giving properties and life-enhancing nature of ... nature. Learning to respect and nurture the land is a good start to understanding the importance of organic practices in the home and in the garden. In the UK the Soil Association is campaigning to educate children by organizing farm visits so that they can learn about safe and wholesome farming methods. Farm visits are a great idea because, straight from the horse's mouth, so to speak, they see how food is grown and processed by organic methods. Strong emphasis is placed on protecting the environment by adopting organic practices.

"Anyone whose heart is in the right place understands that organic by neglect is far different than organic by design."

Joel Salatin

Both on farms and in our own gardens, the starting point for producing good, healthy food will always be a healthy, balanced, living soil. By now we have learnt that the chemicals and toxic compounds—used freely in combating weeds and pests, to fertilize and increase yields—often ultimately reveal themselves in the end to be dangerous to wildlife and humans alike. Their persistence in the soil is still an unknown quantity for many of them and the exact effect of certain chemicals on humans and their offspring is still in debate. By contrast, organic methods have been tried and tested, and although, more often than not, to produce an entirely organic food requires more time and effort, at least we know what we are doing to our soil, our food and the wildlife that we all depend upon.

Where organic farmers lead, organic gardeners follow. But not all farming practices work on the vegetable plot, as I was intrigued to learn on a visit to an organic vegetable farm. Extensive rows of perfectly formed cabbages spread out into the distance, not one blemish or hole was visible, the familiar lacy, bug-infected leaves nowhere to be seen. There were no pests and no damage to the large, healthy leaves. Because there are no chemical fertilizers and no sprays used to rid the crop of insects, the natural balance of nature was allowed to set up home, and in moved the ladybugs and birds, all of which feast upon the insects attracted to the crop—a simple solution with no resulting problems. Protecting homegrown crops is not quite so easy, but methods to encourage wildlife and to extinguish pests are explained in Chapter 3.

> *"The only thing that can save the world is the reclaiming*
> *of the awareness of the world."*
>
> Allen Ginsberg

Change your lifestyle today

Scientists predict that, unless we reduce our impact on the environment NOW, the damage will be irreversible. We are in a perilous state and unless we all react and understand the situation TODAY, we will be leaving our children and our grandchildren a world of chaos, catastrophe and disaster—we cannot guarantee that Mother Nature will look after them. If we are behaving in a greedy and reckless way, the first step to solving the problem is recognizing the fact.
The second step is to do something about it.

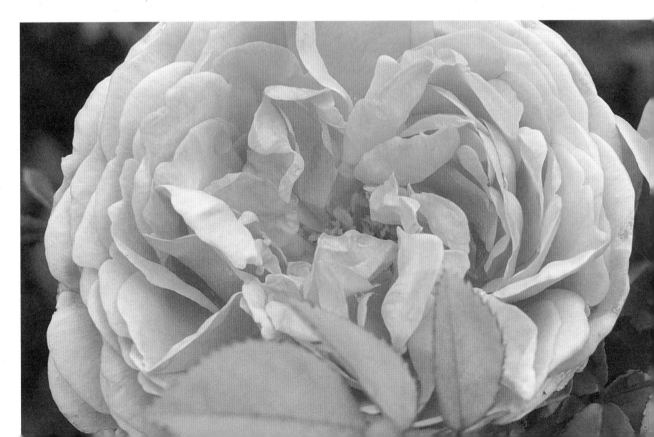

You have bought this book, and hopefully it will make a small difference in your life and a huge difference to the world as we know it.

I am not an authority on housekeeping, gardening, weather patterns, animal husbandry, or science. I know almost nothing about the scientific reasons for global warming and have not the least idea about why we are allowing our governments to get away with NOT DOING VERY MUCH AT ALL ABOUT IT. However, I am a mother and a grandmother. My publishers have been kind enough to ask me to write this book and if it changes 20 lives, or reduces 100lb of carbon footprint it will have been worth the effort. If it introduces 50 more people to the ethics that Cabbages & Roses aspires to, or makes our little company just a bit richer so that we can afford to take our first steps to becoming completely organic, then I shall be happy.

This book is a guide to keeping your house clean by making your own cleaning preparations, growing your own produce and making your own remedies for minor complaints, with the emphasis on doing all these things organically. It encourages us to shop locally, seasonally, and sustainably, supporting farmers and independent storekeepers. If we all adopt this lifestyle, it will have a huge impact on our planet—that of being gentle with it. I have included only the tasks that I perform every year, every month, or every day in this book. None of it is rocket science, but looking at my rituals, my survival techniques and methods of "let's just see if it works," I feel rather pleased that I have learnt how to feed myself, clean myself, and heal myself … organically.

My home is not particularly clean, and the dog and cats live in the kitchen. I am not obsessed with a germfree environment and perhaps it is for this reason that my family is healthy. My garden is doing its best to provide the house with cut flowers, fruit, and vegetables. Even so, I can now see that I must completely change the way I live in order to appease Mother Nature and encourage her to keep her temper and feed my grandchildren.

This book is a very simple, pared down version of all those many expert books on adopting a self-sufficient, organic lifestyle. It is for survival in a greener and more wholesome way. There is enough information to start you on your way and to inspire you to do better, to be better, and to live a better life on a healthier planet.

"We have to move away from a dumb economy that chews up, spits out, and destroys nature and people, towards a smart one that operates with natural cycles: we need to learn to live within our limits."

Dame Anita Roddick

CHAPTER 1

KEEPING HOUSE

In 2003 Greenpeace initiated a "Chemical Home" database. Its aim was to demonstrate that it was possible to substitute safer alternatives for the hazardous chemicals in cleaning materials. By 2006, many manufacturers had indeed found effective and safer alternatives, but there is still a long way to go. In this chapter you will find truly magical alternative cleaning materials, none of which will harm the environment, and all of which are cheap and—most importantly—extremely effective.

Our predilection for chemical antibacterial formulas and overfastidiousness in our homes is, in my opinion, the reason for our seemingly weakened immune systems—I do believe your house can be too clean. Even if you choose to be obsessively clean, try the nonchemical approach for a while and delight in the absence of toxic cleaning materials, on which we all spend too much money and which are really not necessary at all.

Cleaning without chemicals

I have a rather casual approach to keeping house, but whether or not I am tidy, I do make an effort where it matters. This is especially true where food hygiene is concerned—this is one area in my life where I am slightly obsessive.

I rather like cleaning—I am not very good at it, but find it both therapeutic and satisfying. Since I am not as fastidious as I perhaps ought to be, this is definitely a book of "do as I say" or "do as I have recently learned," rather than "do as I do!"

There is little in life more satisfying than tackling a really untidy, unclean room. Starting with the kitchen, I have been finding new ways of dealing with problems that seemed insoluble when all I had to rely on was chemical concoctions that promised to work wonders. In fact, some—most—really don't.

This is by no means a comprehensive advisory chapter on how to keep your house clean. It is merely a hint as to how, by using very few cleaning products, you can achieve most household chores simply, effectively, nontoxically, and safely. I have not covered in detail specialized subjects such as how to dust the frames of priceless paintings (vacuum, covering the nozzle with fine gauze), or how to clean finely carved antique furniture (remove dust with a clean soft paintbrush and use natural beeswax, not aerosol spray polish). This is just a very simple, ordinary, day-to-day list of general housekeeping equipment, cleaning products, and techniques.

DISPOSABLE WIPES
These wipes are not environmentally friendly. Use them only in emergency situations, perhaps keeping a packet in the car. The rest of the time water and cloth will do the same job—on picnics, for example, take a glass bottle of water and some recycled cloths with you.

RIGHT: *With only two vital cleaning products required for most household tasks, you can keep them easily accessible.*

The cleaning cupboard

This is a list of the housekeeping equipment and cleaning products that I find useful. I have no need for anything more.

Beeswax polish (see page 32)

Baking soda (Bicarbonate of soda), in industrial quantities
(see pages 28–30)

Borax Substitute (see page 32)

Chamois leather, for cleaning windows and rubbing off pet hair

Distilled white vinegar, in industrial quantities
(see pages 22–27)

Natural, ready-prepared cleaning fluids and detergent powder (such as Ecover)

Enamel buckets—a good selection, preferably vintage. Why buy new ones when so many are available from flea markets and secondhand stores?

Feather or lambswool duster with a long handle for reaching cobwebs and behind furniture

Jam jars with screw lids

Lemons, for various cleaning purposes

Muslin, for food covers, straining jelly, etc.

Old toothbrushes, for cleaning awkward corners

Rags, for use as cleaning cloths. Make these from worn-out cotton dresses and T-shirts, towels, dish towels, and bed linens that are beyond mending. Cut the cloth into squares. Wash or boil used rags regularly. You may never need to buy another dustcloth; most people have enough rags to last a lifetime.

Refillable spray bottles

Soda crystals

Washing line and wooden clothespins (clothes pegs)

Wooden bristle scrubbing brush

Wooden-handled, bristle-brushed brooms (these last forever, unlike their plastic counterparts). A hard-bristle brush is best for outdoor use and a soft-bristle brush for indoor sweeping.

Wooden-handled, small bristle brush with tin dustpan (plastic is not eco-friendly and is breakable). As above, a soft-bristle brush is best for indoors while a hard-bristle brush removes dried mud and other dirt from carpets and rugs.

LEFT: *Jam jars with screw lids and kilner jars are useful for all manner of things, from homemade jam to storing dustcloth (dusters) dipped in lemon oil, or for keeping leftovers in the fridge.*

lemon dustcloths (Dusters)

Whether you are using bought dustcloths or cutting up old cotton clothes, towels, or dish towels (tea towels) to serve the purpose, with this method you can clean your furniture without resorting to spray polish. Prepare several dustcloths at a time, and store them until needed. Make sure you wash or boil the dustcloths regularly after use and re-infuse them with lemon and oil.

you will need

Water
White distilled vinegar
Lemon oil or olive oil
Dustcloths or rags
Lemons
Airtight jar with screw lid

1 Make a solution of two parts water, two parts vinegar, and two drops of lemon oil or olive oil. Soak your dustcloths or rags in this solution and squeeze out the excess, leaving them just damp.

2 Pare the rind from several lemons, depending how many rags you are preparing, and lay a couple of pieces on each smoothed-out dustcloth.

3 Fold each one, or roll it up, and store in a clean jam jar with an extra piece of lemon peel. The jar should be airtight with a screw lid.

White distilled vinegar

For 10,000 years this fermented alcohol (most probably accidentally stumbled upon) has had hundreds of different uses. The Babylonians discovered its preserving properties; the Romans drank it; the Greeks pickled vegetables and meats in it; and soldiers during the American Civil War used it to treat scurvy. It heals wounds, cleans glass, and melts away limescale and grease.

For the recipes in this chapter use only white distilled vinegar. Once you realize how useful it is, you will probably want to stock up on several gallons of this magical liquid!

Altered hem and seam lines

If you mind about holes left after taking down a hem or re-sewing a seam, iron the fabric over a cloth dampened with vinegar.

Baby clothes

To freshen baby clothes, add one cup of vinegar to the detergent (washing powder) dispenser of the washing machine for the final rinse cycle. This will break down the uric acid and soapy residue on the clothes, leaving them soft and fresh. (You may also want to do this to liven up tired fabrics.)

Blankets

To wash wool or cotton blankets, add two cups of vinegar to the rinse cycle. This will make them soft, fluffy, and free of soap.

Boiled eggs

To prevent an egg from leaking from its shell while it is being boiled, add a splash of vinegar to the water.

LEFT: *Adding a drop of vinegar to the cooking water will stop eggshells from leaking.*

RIGHT: *Keep a permanent washing line strung up in a spare room or laundry, and use it to dry clothes when the weather is inclement.*

Brass, copper, and pewter

To make an effective polish, mix one teaspoon of salt and one cup of vinegar, stirring in enough flour to make a paste. Cover the item with the paste and leave for 15 minutes. Wash off with warm water and polish with a soft dry cloth.

Burn marks

Rub neat vinegar onto the fabric with a soft cloth, then rinse with water. (Test on an inconspicuous area first.)

Carpet stains

Blot spills as soon as possible with a paper towel. For a stain, mix one teaspoon of Ecover dishwashing liquid with one teaspoon of vinegar dissolved in $2^{1}/_{2}$ cups (about half a liter) of lukewarm water. Apply to the stain with a soft cloth and rub gently. Rinse with warm water and blot dry.

Cigarette odors

To remove the odor of cigar or cigarette smoke, leave a saucer of vinegar in the room overnight.

Cooking odors

To rid the kitchen of cooking odors, simmer a solution of vinegar and water in a pan for 5 minutes.

Cut flowers

To keep cut flowers fresh for longer, add two teaspoons of sugar and two tablespoons of vinegar to the flower water. Trim the stems and change the water every five days.

Deodorant stains

To remove deodorant stains on colored clothes, rub with a soft cloth dipped in vinegar and wash as usual.

LEFT: *Keep glossy copper pots in prime condition by cleaning with a paste made from vinegar, salt, and flour.*

Drains

To deodorize drains, pour a cup of vinegar down the drain and leave for half an hour, then flush through with running cold water. A mixture of vinegar and baking soda will do the job even more thoroughly. Pour two tablespoons of baking soda down the sink hole followed by half a cup of vinegar, leave to bubble for 20 minutes, then flush through by running the cold faucet (tap) for a minute.

Dyeing fabric

When dyeing fabrics, add a tablespoon of vinegar to the final rinse to help set the color.

Fish

When steaming, poaching, or baking fish, first soak it in vinegar and water for half an hour. This will keep the flesh from crumbling and make it tender and sweeter to taste. Rinse in cold water, then cook.

Fruit stains on hands

Clean fruit-stained hands with neat vinegar.

Insect pests

If you have trouble with insects (silverfish, ants, etc.) wipe down kitchen surfaces with neat vinegar to deter visits. This will also disinfect the surfaces.

Iron plate stains

Mix one part vinegar with one part salt, and heat gently in a small pan. Rub the solution onto the cold iron plate to remove stains. Wipe clean with a damp cloth.

Leather

Mix one part vinegar with two parts linseed oil then use a soft cloth to rub the solution into the leather. Buff with a clean cloth. (Test on an inconspicuous area first.)

RIGHT: *Vintage linen dish towels can be soaked in vinegar and water to remove stains and lengthen their life.*

Lime deposits in showerhead

If the showerhead is clogged with lime deposits, soak in a bowl of one part vinegar to three parts water. Check after 30 minutes and rinse in clean cold water.

Lime deposits on faucets (taps)

To rid faucets of lime deposits, soak a terry-cloth rag in vinegar, then wrap it around the faucets and areas of buildup. Leave for half an hour, then rinse clean.

Microwave ovens

To clean and deodorize a microwave oven, fill a microwaveable bowl with vinegar, and boil in the oven. This will loosen dried food on the walls, which can then be wiped clean with a soft, damp cloth.

Paintbrushes

To soften stiff paintbrushes, soak the bristles in hot vinegar. Rinse with clean, soapy water before using.

Painted walls and woodwork

Make a solution of two parts vinegar, one part baking soda, and three parts warm water. Dip a soft cloth into the solution and use it to wipe the dirt from surfaces; rinse with clean water.

Potatoes

To keep peeled potatoes white, add a teaspoon of vinegar to the water they are soaking in until they are cooked.

Red wine stains

Blot the stain immediately with a soft, dry cloth, and sponge with undiluted vinegar until it is gone.

Refrigerators

Clean the inside of the refrigerator with a solution made from equal parts of vinegar and water.

Ring marks on wooden furniture

To remove ring marks on wooden furniture, make a solution of one part vinegar and one part olive oil. Use a soft cloth to rub the ring mark with the solution, then polish with natural beeswax.

Rinsing fresh produce

To freshen salads and vegetables, or to clean chemical residue from store-bought nonorganic fresh produce, soak in cold water to which you have added two tablespoons of vinegar. Rinse after soaking.

Rust stains

Remove rust stains on delicate fabrics with a mixture of vinegar and hot water. Dab the spot gently with the solution on a clean cloth until the rust is removed. (Another traditional method

LEFT: *Wooden chopping boards will last much longer than a lifetime. Lemons will clean and disinfect them.*

of removing rust stains or iron mold from delicate fabrics is to soak the item in the juice of cooked rhubarb, then rinse in clean warm water.)

Sink garbage disposal units

To clean a sink waste disposal unit, make ice cubes with one part vinegar and one part water. Put the cubes into the unit and switch on. This spatters the vinegar cubes throughout the system. Flush the unit with cold water afterward.

Stale odors

To remove stale odors lurking in cookie tins or lunch boxes, dip a slice of fresh bread in vinegar and leave in the tin or box overnight.

Steam irons

To remove lime deposits from steam irons, mix equal quantities of vinegar and distilled water and fill the water chamber. Heat the iron for 5 minutes, then press the steam button over scrap fabric to rid the chamber of the lime deposits. When cool, tip out the solution. Rinse the chamber well.

Toilet bowl staining

To freshen up the toilet and remove stubborn stains, spray neat vinegar around the bowl and brush clean. Leave to soak overnight, if necessary.

Windows

Make a solution of one part vinegar and one part warm water. Pour into a spray bottle, then spray onto glass. Rub the glass dry with a soft cloth, then polish with crumpled newspaper for a sheen.

Wooden chopping boards

Vinegar or lemon juice will clean, deodorize, and disinfect wooden chopping boards. These are more ecologically sound than plastic ones.

RIGHT: *Windows can be made sparklingly clear with just vinegar and old newspaper.*

Baking soda (Bicarbonate of soda)

This is another miracle of nature. Most baking soda is made from trona ore, mined from natural deposits throughout the world, but predominantly found in Wyoming. Baking soda can be manufactured and is formed by combining carbonic acid and sodium hydroxide. Trona, however, is a naturally occurring substance, which is easily mined, and it is the source of most baking soda.

Trona was discovered in the mid 1840s. Then, as now, it was used by many households for scouring, cleaning, and deodorizing. Trona, or baking soda, is also known as bicarbonate of soda and sodium bicarbonate. It is best known for its uses in cooking, becoming a raising agent when it is mixed with cream of tartar.

Brass

To clean brass, make a paste of baking soda and lemon juice. Apply and leave for a minute, then rinse well.

Carpets

Sprinkle baking soda over carpets to deodorize them. Leave for an hour, then vacuum.

Chrome

For polishing chrome, make a paste of baking soda and water. Rinse thoroughly with clean water to remove deposits.

Cooking cabbage

To keep cabbage bright green during cooking, add a pinch of baking soda to the water. This helps the leaves to retain their magnesium.

Cut flowers

Add a pinch of baking soda to cut-flower water to keep it fresher for longer. This works as well as the sugar and vinegar solution (see page 24).

Dishcloths (tea towels) and washcloths (face flannels)

Soak dishcloths and washcloths in a strong solution of baking soda and water to freshen them up.

Garbage cans (Dustbins)

Sprinkle baking soda into the bottom of garbage cans to remove unpleasant odors. After emptying the garbage, add some water and swill around the can. Pour it out and leave to dry, then add more baking soda for next time.

LEFT: *Use baking soda instead of a multitude of chemical cleaning products.*

RIGHT: *Cut flowers will last longer if a pinch of baking soda is dissolved in the water.*

Glass decanters

To clean the hard-to-reach inside of a glass decanter, make a solution of baking soda, crushed dry eggshells, and warm water. Swish around in the decanter and leave overnight. Rinse well with white distilled vinegar to remove the residue, then rinse thoroughly with warm water.

Hairbrushes and combs

Make a solution of baking soda and warm water. Soak hairbrushes and combs for an hour to remove dirt and grease, then rinse with warm water.

Kitchens and bathrooms

When mixed with water, baking soda makes an alkaline solution that will cut through grease and dirt on most surfaces in kitchens and bathrooms. Used dry, it is effective as an abrasive powder; mixed with distilled white vinegar, it becomes even more powerful.

Laundry

To reduce the amount of detergent powder (washing powder) used for each laundry load and to make it more effective, it's a good idea to substitute baking soda for half the normal dose. (Detergent powder contains far fewer chemicals than its liquid equivalents.)

Mattress stains

To remove mattress stains, make a loose paste of with baking soda and water, and apply it to the stain. Leave to dry so that the powder disperses into the mattress, then brush off the residue. The baking soda will also deodorize the mattress.

Mildew on shower curtains

To remove mildew growing on shower curtains, apply a paste of baking soda and water. Leave on the curtain overnight and wash off the next day with warm water.

Oven cleaning

After cleaning the oven, make a light paste of baking soda and water. Use it to brush inside the oven and you will find that cleaning is much easier next time.

Refrigerator odours

Keep a saucer of baking soda inside the fridge to absorb and remove food odors, replacing it every two weeks. And instead of throwing away the old baking soda, pour it into the kitchen sink, followed by a kettle of boiling water to keep drains fresh and odor-free.

Rust on cooking utensils

Dip the cut edge of a potato into a saucer of baking soda and rub over the rust. Rinse the utensil, then wipe it with a cloth dipped in a little olive oil to prevent the rust from forming again.

Silver

To clean silver, soak it in boiling water with baking soda, cream of tartar, salt, and a piece of aluminum foil.

Stains inside cups and teapots

Fill the items with a solution of baking soda and water. Leave until the staining disappears, then rinse. For stubborn stains, use a solution of baking soda and white distilled vinegar.

RIGHT: *A tried-and-tested method for cleaning glass decanters is to use a mixture of crushed eggshells, baking soda, and warm water.*

Borax substitute

An extremely effective antibacterial, fungicidal, cleaning, and bleaching agent, borax substitute is almost as effective as normal commercial bleach. It is, however, a healthier option for the environment. It has low toxicity for people, though higher toxicity for animals.

Carpet stains

Mix the borax substitute with a little water into a paste. Test on an unexposed area of carpet for color fastness, then rub into the stain, allow to dry, and vacuum off the powder. For wine and other liquid stains, dissolve half a cup of borax substitute in 2 cups (about half a liter) of warm water. Rub into the stain, leave for 30 minutes, and sponge off. For odors, dampen the area, sprinkle with borax substitute, leave to dry, and then vacuum.

Laundry

Add half a cup of borax substitute to your wash load with the usual amount of detergent powder (washing powder) to boost its cleaning power and deodorize the wash.

Refrigerators

Dissolve one tablespoon of borax substitute in a 4 cups (about a liter) of warm water and use to wipe the fridge clean and deodorize it at the same time.

Washing delicate items

Soak in a solution of half a cup of borax substitute with one or two tablespoons of detergent powder (washing powder) in a bowl of warm water. Rinse in cool water, and dry as appropriate.

RIGHT: *Use a vintage enamel pail to soak delicate items in a solution of borax substitute and warm water.*

Beeswax

Making your own beeswax polish is simple, but potentially very dangerous, as the ingredients—pure beeswax and turpentine—are extremely flammable. They do not boil but become hotter and hotter until they catch fire. The flash point is low, and burning beeswax is particularly difficult to extinguish. This is why I suggest you buy natural beeswax polish instead of making it.

For cleaning wood furniture, beeswax is infinitely preferable to the polish sold in aerosol cans and containing silicone. Spray polishes create a shiny, impenetrable surface, whereas beeswax feeds the wood, giving it a luxurious, deep, well-fed shine. It is not necessary to polish furniture more than about four or five times a year, provided it is kept dusted. (For intricately carved pieces of furniture or picture frames, a soft, fat, clean paintbrush can be used to remove dust from tricky corners.) An alternative to beeswax is a drop of olive oil. This will feed the wood and, when buffed with a soft cloth, produce a lovely natural shine.

Kitchen hygiene

All kitchen surfaces and wooden chopping boards should be kept as clean as possible, using any of the ingredients listed on pages 22–32 or ecologically safe and sound brands.

I feel our dependence on antibacterial substances has made us a tad lazy in the kitchen hygiene department. It is not necessary to rely on chemicals to keep our kitchens clean and to avoid food poisoning. Common sense and an awareness of the dangers contained in raw meat, fish, and some other foods should keep you and your family safe and healthy. Thorough cooking of foods at high enough temperatures, cleanliness, hand washing, and the avoidance of cross contamination are all essential if you are to avoid causing illness.

Wash hands and surfaces thoroughly after handling raw meat, and keep all raw meats on a covered plate at the bottom of the refrigerator.

Dry your hands on a towel kept purely for that purpose, and do not be tempted to use the same towel to dry dishes. Change dishcloths and dish towels (tea towels) every day. Keep them clean by boiling them regularly in a solution of water and white distilled vinegar with a teaspoon of baking soda. This is especially important after using them with raw meat and fish.

RIGHT: *Keep separate towels for drying hands and dishes, to avoid any cross contamination.*

Chopping boards

Although we were led to believe that plastic boards were safer than their wooden counterparts, research carried out by microbiologists at the University of Wisconsin's Food Research Institute in 1993 proved otherwise. Testing the theory that wood contained antibacterial properties, in a controlled experiment they intentionally contaminated both types of chopping board with bacteria responsible for food poisoning. Their study showed that germs placed on the wooden chopping board died within three minutes, but the bacteria on the plastic board not only remained alive but multiplied overnight.

The explanation for these incredible results is that wood has natural antibacterial properties. The capillary action of dry wood causes germs to disappear quickly beneath the surface of the board, where they soon die, leaving the exposed dry area free from microbes. In contrast, the smooth, impenetrable surface of the plastic board hosted germs comfortably. Where the board has been scarred by knives, the germs are there to stay and multiply.

In spite of these findings, it is important that you never assume that wooden chopping boards decontaminate themselves. Hand-washing or scrubbing both types of board thoroughly with soap and hot water will kill most dangerous germs. However, after chopping raw chicken, make sure you scrub with plenty of soap and boiling water. Air-dry wooden chopping boards and never put them in the dishwasher.

To disinfect both wooden and plastic boards, spray with white distilled vinegar, leave for half an hour, then rinse. For many reasons, it is always preferable to use wooden rather than plastic chopping boards.

Some manufacturers claim that their antibacterial plastic chopping boards are self-sanitizing. These claims are untrue—it is not possible to produce plastic that is inherently antibacterial.

In short, opt for our grandmothers' choice of chopping board: good old-fashioned wood, scrubbed clean with a bristle brush. A sensible precaution is to keep boards used for bread and vegetables separate from those used for meat.

RIGHT: *This glass cover is beautiful enough for the table. A wire dome covering is also extremely practical, allowing air to circulate but keeping flies away.*

BELOW: *Have plenty of wooden chopping boards, and make sure all members of the household know which to use just for meat.*

Food covers

To research the safety of plastic wrap (clingfilm), I contacted the United Kingdom's Food Standards Agency. Their website advises that plastic wrap is safe if used correctly, and that not every plastic wrap is safe for all uses. They make the following recommendations, which are aimed at protecting the quality and taste of food from easily avoidable migration from plastic wraps, and preventing inappropriate use of wraps:

▶ Do not use plastic wraps where they might melt into the food, such as in conventional ovens or with pots and pans on burners.

▶ When reheating or cooking food in a microwave oven, make sure that the plastic wrap does not touch the food.

▶ Use plastic wrap in contact with high-fat foods *only* when the manufacturer's advice states it is suitable for this. Examples of high-fat foods include some types of cheese, raw meats with a layer of fat, fried meats, pastry products, and cakes with butter icing or chocolate coatings.

Similar cautions have been expressed by the United States Food and Drug Administration. My opinion is that if it is necessary for a product to carry any warning at all, it should be avoided. Although the Food Standards Agency states that plastic wrap is safe when used correctly, I can only presume that it is unsafe when used incorrectly. I asked the Agency what the effects and/or dangers are in using plastic wrap on certain types of food. They simply reiterated the instruction to avoid using it with fatty foods. When pressed on the point, the Agency advisor could/would not expand on what harm is done by inappropriate use of plastic wrap. I was assured that by law all packaging of plastic wrap had to carry a warning, but clingfilm is not the right covering to use.

Since writing this in 2007, it has come to light that harmful substances are used in making clingfilm, including the chemical Bisphenol A (BPA). Beeswax food wraps are an excellent alternative. These are pieces of cotton that have been infused with beeswax, making them reusable and breathable, as well as eco-friendly. When warmed by the hands, beeswax wraps become sticky, making it easy to cover bowls and wrap food such as sandwiches.

Alternative food covers

Infinitely preferable to plastic wrap are reuseable food covers. There is a multitude of options, including wire, netting, glass, and fabric—simple muslin is something often forgotten about. An upturned plate will suffice for cooling a dish before putting it into the fridge. And don't forget about using good old-fashioned wax paper, particularly for wrapping sandwiches—string or a rubber band will keep it in place.

Sell-by dates

I cannot imagine how much profit is made by supermarkets and food producers from "sell-by dates." I am guilty of blindly following date guidance, because I am from a generation that has always believed that big business knows best. While I cannot categorically say that sell-by dates are a bad thing, it is a convenient and slightly sneaky way to encourage people to dispose of and buy more food. For some time (most of my adult life, actually) I have erred on the side of caution rather than using my own natural senses, instinct, and sense of self-preservation. Yet by using your sense of smell and your eyesight, and by buying from suppliers you trust, you will save a fortune by not throwing away food merely because the packaging tells you to do so.

Determining food freshness

Eggs One thing that is often difficult to judge by its "use-by" date is an egg. A simple test for freshness is to place the egg in a glass of water. If it sinks to the bottom of the glass, it is fresh enough to use, but if it floats, do not use it.

Fruit and vegetables Provided that they are not excessively packaged, it is simple to determine the freshness of fruit and vegetables. They should be firm and brightly colored. If they are not of perfect shape or have slight blemishes, use your common sense to judge whether they are edible or not. Sadly, we have been dictated to by nonsensical laws governing the suitable shape of our vegetables—a bent carrot or a straight banana will have no relevance to its taste or freshness.

Local traders If you live in a town where there are good small, independent food shopkeepers—such as a butcher, a fishmonger, a delicatessen—give them your patronage and build up a good relationship with them. Judge their hygiene standards by your own. Let them know if anything you buy from them is disappointing or actually contaminated—or if it's especially delicious. You'll find that shopping becomes more of a pleasure than it is in the faceless, homogenized atmosphere of the supermarket.

BELOW: *Before using eggs in your recipes, check their freshness by seeing if they sink in a glass of water.*

Recycling in the kitchen

As much as you can, try to avoid buying food that has been excessively packaged. This is much simpler if you shop locally, at farmers' markets or specialist food shops. When you do use the supermarket, opt for loose vegetables rather than the prepackaged varieties that come in plastic trays covered with more, impossible-to-unwrap plastic, then sold in a plastic bag.

In recent years, the brown paper grocery bags traditionally used in American supermarkets have been increasingly replaced by plastic bags. Millions of these are simply thrown away, rather than recycled. You might think that paper bags are a more eco-friendly option; but their manufacture involves the destruction of huge areas of forest (typically 14 million trees annually in the United States alone) and the use of toxic chemicals.

The solution is to reuse any bags you are given as many times as possible and, even better, to equip yourself with some permanent shopping bags, made of cloth or string. Keep some handy in your car. A large basket is useful for carrying just a few purchases.

RIGHT: *Baskets and fabric shoppers are preferable to, and much more beautiful than, plastic shopping bags.*

Reducing packaging

Buy in bulk wherever possible, and you can avoid having to throw away at least half of the usual amount of packaging used for smaller units. If you have the space to store dry goods that won't deteriorate with age (such as bathroom tissue, distilled vinegar, baking soda, borax substitute, Epsom salts, detergent powder), buy them in sufficient quantities to last three months. Having a stock of these bulky items will lighten the load when you're shopping for food and may even allow you to do some of those trips on foot.

One of the few modern-day inventions that can make up for their carbon footprint in usefulness is the freezer. Well stocked and efficiently run, it can save many a trip to the supermarket, and is invaluable for storing seasonal fruit and vegetables from the garden or market, to keep you fed throughout the winter months.

Local government recycling schemes

Recycle glass, cans, foil, and plastic, and compost all uncooked vegetable matter (see pages 72–77). Local governments offer recycling schemes, so contact them to find out how you should go about recycling. In Britain, the issue has become quite contentious, with the "carrot" being replaced by the "stick." There's talk of penalties for failing to recycle, even of garbage cans equipped with cameras to monitor what is thrown into them.

If governments are truly concerned about recycling, they will make it simple for us to do. One clear rule would be a good start. Tell us what to do and we will do it. Make it easy for us to do, and we will do it with pleasure.

Recycled china

I can think of nothing prettier than a dresser full of mismatched vintage china. I can think of little more dull than a dresser full of matching china. Not only is mismatched china cheaper, more interesting, and a beautiful exercise in recycling, it saves the problem of finding or replacing a piece of china from a discontinued range. If you start in a muddle, you can continue in a muddle and make a beautiful display of it.

Avoid buying cracked or chipped china if it is to be used in cooking or for food, but pieces that are less than perfect can be used as ashtrays, soap dishes, or bowls for fragrant pot pourri. Cups can be filled with candle wax and given away as gifts (see page 176).

If you use a dishwasher, make sure that everyday china is dishwasher proof, or you might find that the patterns fade to nothing over time. My vintage china is rarely used, but when it is I wash it by hand.

Keep glass, both old and new, gleaming with recipes using vinegar and other concoctions listed on pages 18–20.

RIGHT: *Mis-matched china makes an interesting display on the open shelves of a kitchen dresser.*

Household pests

Every household has its share of uninvited visitors, especially if you have pets sharing your space. Our normal reaction is to turn to toxic commercial pesticides, which may well do more harm than good. Unless your problem is extreme, natural, nontoxic alternatives will deal with most problems.

Start by deterring pests from moving into your home in the first place. Seal cracks and holes; and if a hole is too inconvenient to fill, prevent rats and mice from entering by filling the gap with steel wool. This is one of the few materials that even rats won't bother to gnaw through. Another expedient is a humane trap, which allows the rodent to be released into the wild. However, rats are quite a big pest to deal with; so, personally, I would call in the professionals if you are unfortunate enough to have a problem.

Ants

If you are plagued with ants inside the house, the first thing to establish is where they are coming from and why. Remove the crumbs or food sources that are tempting them. Wipe surfaces with distilled white vinegar or pure lemon juice. At the point of entry, lay any of the following deterrents: cayenne pepper; cinnamon; citrus oil; cloves; sliced cloves of fresh garlic; crushed dried lemon peel; lemon juice; dried mint leaves; and, curiously, cucumber peel.

Cockroaches

These unsightly creatures often live at high levels; so when using deterrents, don't forget to spray above cabinets and shelves. Simmer catnip sachets in water to make a solution to spray on areas infested by cockroaches. They dislike soapy water; so if you do suffer an infestation in your home, keep a spray bottle filled with a strong solution of soap and water handy, as this will kill them. Borax substitute dissolved in water in a spray bottle will also kill these horrid pests. Other deterrents include bay leaves, garlic, and sliced cucumber. Nontoxic cockroach traps are available .

KEEPING RODENTS AT BAY
Once a month, use peppermint oil in your floor cleaning water to ward off rodents. Keep a refillable spray bottle filled with a strong mixture of water and peppermint oil to spray around the outside of garbage cans, in the attic, and in the backs of closets.

PETS AND PESTS

Animal parasites

To deter ticks and fleas on cats and dogs, add about a teaspoon of vinegar to your pet's water bowl. As a guide, for a 40lb (18kg) creature (dog, not a flea!) add one teaspoon per approximately 1 quart (1 liter) of water.

Puppy accidents

To prevent puppy accidents from staining carpets, sprinkle with neat vinegar (test for colorfastness in an inconspicuous area) and blot with clean absorbent cloth or paper towel. Repeat if necessary. This treatment will also prevent odors.

Fleas on pets

These are a constant problem, especially in the summer months. Adding distilled white vinegar or apple cider vinegar to your pet's drinking water will act as a deterrent. Washing pets regularly with mild soap to which you have added the juice of a lemon will also keep the little beasts at bay.

Dip a comb in a solution made from boiling water poured onto lemon slices, wait until cool, then comb your pet with the lemon water to act as a further deterrent. If you trap fleas on the comb, drown them in soapy water immediately by immersing the comb into a prepared bowl.

Cedar shampoo and cedar oil can also be used in the fight against flea infestation. Make a solution of water, vinegar, and cedar oil. Keep this in a spray bottle and spray pet bedding regularly to keep fleas away. Make a pocket from muslin, fill it with a mixture of cedar chips, lavender, and lemon peel, and place it under the bedding inside pet baskets. Change the mixture every month or so to keep it fresh and effective.

Keep carpets and areas under furniture well vacuumed; and if you know fleas have been present, empty the vacuum bag every time you use it, sealing and disposing of the contents carefully outside.

RIGHT: *It's far better to keep your pet pest-free by using natural remedies, instead of harsh chemicals.*

Dust mites

These ever-present microscopic creatures are not such a problem unless someone in your household has an allergic reaction or suffers from asthma. If so, seek medical advice; but really the only way to deal with mites is to be scrupulous with vacuuming. Pay special attention to mattresses, fabric-covered headboards, and pillows. Keep furniture, books, throws, and rugs dust free by vacuuming. Seal the vacuum bag tightly and dispose of it carefully. If possible, air items and beat throws, blankets, duvets, and rugs outside in the fresh air. Hang the items on a line outside and thwack—if you can't find a carpet beater, an old tennis racket will do. Washing bedding regularly at the "extra hot" setting should rid bedding of mites.

Mosquitoes

Mosquitoes are a horrible fact of life, especially if you live near still water. There are many commercial, nontoxic preparations available, but the following will also deter them.

Mix one part garlic juice with five parts water and keep in a spray bottle. Shake well before use, then spray onto exposed parts of the body. To prevent mosquitoes from entering the house, hang strips of cotton cloth dipped into this solution at open windows; or, if you have screens, spray these with the solution. For outside eating areas, surround the table with marigold, rosemary, and sage plants. Avoid still water—bird baths, still ponds, and puddles—near social areas. For sleeping, a mosquito net hung over the bed is the best natural deterrent available.

Moths

Once moths have set up home, it is extremely difficult to persuade them to leave. One of the best lines of defense is to be scrupulous in your vacuuming, paying special attention to the edges of rooms and underneath furniture and rugs. The second defense is to be extremely vigilant when buying old and imported furniture, rugs, natural floor coverings, and secondhand or vintage clothing. These are often the origin of an infestation.

Natural moth deterrents include
- aromatic cedar chips
- bay leaves
- dried lemon peel
- lavender
- rosemary
- rose petals

All these natural ingredients can be combined into an attractive, fragrant pot pourri (as the Elizabethans did) and displayed in bowls placed in strategic positions around the house. Alternatively, you can make muslin pockets, fill them with some of the ingredients, and tie with string. Even having taken all precautions in avoidance of moths, you will find that vigilance is still the most important thing you can practise.

If you do find yourself with a moth problem, soak porous string in cedar, lavender, or rosemary oil, then trail this around the edges of the room between the wall and the edge of the carpet. Make sure the string is not wet or saturated when you lay it, as it may stain the carpet; first leave it to drip outside so that it is infused but not wet.

MOTHBALLS
Avoid chemically made mothballs, since they contain naphthalene, which can be fatal to small children and pets. They also have a musty, unpleasant odor, which will permeate your clothes and be very difficult to get rid of.

FOOD MOTHS
These are found in dry goods such as flour and cereals. Like mice, they can chew their way into cardboard and paper packaging, but unlike mice, they are tiny and difficult to detect.

Make sure you clean out your pantry (larder) regularly and vacuum the corners of the room where they are likely to be entering. Decant dry goods from packets into sealed containers, and keep a watchful eye.

sticky fly paper

These homemade devices are wonderful for trapping all types of flying insects and infinitely preferable to toxic fly sprays. The paper can be changed as soon as it becomes disturbingly full—a fly paper at full capacity is not an attractive sight.

Make several at a time and hang them strategically around the kitchen, or wherever you have a flying insect problem. A word of warning, though—do not make the mistake of hanging them where passing people might get their hair caught. I have known this to happen and I cannot think of anything worse than having this sticky contraption tangled in your hair!

you will need

Strong brown paper
Scissors
Hole puncher
String
Saucepan
Water
Sugar
Honey or corn syrup
Baking tray

1 Cut some strips of tough brown paper. Make a hole at the top of each strip so that you can thread a length of string through it to form a hanging loop.

2 In a saucepan, mix one part water, one part sugar, and one part honey or corn syrup, and heat until the mixture has combined well. Turn off the heat and allow the mixture to cool a little.

3 Dip each paper strip into the syrup mixture, making sure each side is well coated.

4 Suspend the strips over a baking tray and leave to drip. When dry, the sticky fly papers are ready to hang up in place.

The closet

At the forefront of the news headlines in recent months, in Britain, is the exposure of unscrupulous manufacturers flouting employment laws and behaving in Machiavellian ways, paying low wages and sometimes no wages at all to the most vulnerable people in the workplace. Providing appalling working conditions, these manufacturers force unnaturally long hours on their workers and impose contracts that tie them to their workplace, sometimes for life. Children are among the most vulnerable, employed in factories where they work for as much as 10 hours a day, often in poorly ventilated and dangerous conditions.

According to the charity Triad, which specializes in recycling textiles, about 900,000 tons of clothing and shoes are thrown away every year. Up to 95% of these items could be recycled. We are buying so much that 75 percent of it ends up in landfill after less than 6 months. The US Environment Protection Agency reports that Americans throw away an average of 68 lb (31kg) of clothing and textiles per person per year. Even thrift shops are experiencing a glut of cast-offs.

Consider where and how clothes have been made. It is becoming easier to source organic, or at least fair-trade, fabrics, and designers are more aware that the provenance of their garments is as important as their appearance. We will always be influenced by the price of new clothes, but it is more important to be aware of their value—not because of a designer label, but because of how the garment has been made and what it has been made from. Probably the best advice I can offer is to be aware of what you are buying:

- Be aware of social justice.
- Buy good-quality clothing for a fair price.
- Buy one good piece for every 10 cheap pieces you might have bought in the past, and look after it.

As part of this new regime, spend time on finding clothes that will last, that are of good quality and cut, and that will suit your lifestyle. Turn your back on fashion fads—by which I mean anything that will embarrass you or your children in two years' time. A good starting point is to sort out your existing wardrobe.

Matching hangers

Begin with matching hangers. A well-organized, presentable wardrobe will make life a million times easier, and it will be a pleasure to choose from. During the early days at Cabbages & Roses we acquired wire hangers from our local dry cleaners at no cost, and spent many a happy hour binding them with the white waste selvedges of our fabrics. Ranks of white bound hangers made a very pleasing display—it was an extremely cheap and useful reclamation exercise. The clothes never slipped off the dry cotton, which transformed harsh wire into a chic display at no cost. If you haven't the time or inclination to sit covering wire hangers for hours (even bearing in mind the therapeutic benefits of the task), just make sure all the hangers in your closet are the same—this is important for a calm, coordinated, easy-to-choose-from display, something you will be grateful for when getting dressed in a hurry.

BELOW: *Matching clothes hangers make for an orderly closet.*

patching clothes

When a hole or tear appears in a favorite item of clothing, try patching it. The patch should be of the same, or similar, material as that of the garment, but as for color and pattern—that all depends on what you can lay your hands on and your imagination. So long as they are complementary rather than clashing, choose whatever fabric you like.

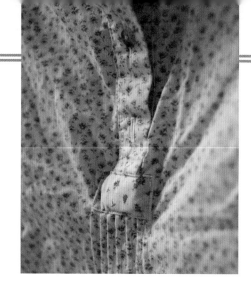

you will need

Fabric of suitable color and pattern
Needle and thread to match fabric
Scissors
Pins

1 Measure the tear in the garment and cut out a square or rectangular piece of fabric that allows enough to cover it plus a surplus of 2in. (5cm) on each side.

2 On the wrong side, turn over about ½in. (1cm) on each side and sew, neatly folding in the corners.

3 Then turn over ½in. (1cm) and sew, again neatly folding in the corners. The cut edges of the patch are thus turned in, which prevents fraying.

4 Position the patch on the garment, secure with pins, and then sew neatly in place.

Sorting your clothes

Rearrange your clothes. If you haven't worn something for two years, get rid of it. In my experience it is a huge muddle of too many clothes that leads a woman's brain to believe that she has nothing to wear and to get overwhelmed by the urge to buy more, only adding to the muddle. Certainly, I could manage with 10 pieces of clothing. I shall "cull and consolidate" and urge you to do the same.

It is far better to have a few perfect items than to have hundreds of cheap ones. Just as in growing your own food, having less makes one appreciate what one does have. Assuming that you will be left only with things that you love, it will be much easier to spend time repairing, reviving, and perhaps remodeling them.

This is also a very good reason/excuse to go and buy proper clothes from proper shops. Choose beautiful garments that will fill you with glee for at least the next five years. If five T-shirts can be bought for $5.00, £5.00, or 5 euros, you can bet your bottom dollar (£, euro) that someone, somewhere is NOT benefiting.

Recycling clothes

In the enormous sort-out that you are about to do/already have done, reuse, and recycle as much as you can. Old T-shirts can be cut up and used as dustcloths, and pantyhose can be cut up and used as bags to fill with lavender. Pantyhose also make a very good plant tie, so keep a stock of them handy.

Recycle by organizing a clothes swap with your friends—one woman's big mistake is another woman's heavenly new dress/coat/skirt. If you have exhausted all avenues of disposal (thrift (charity) shops, friends, children), take your old clothes to a recycling center.

Mending

If a button on a garment is missing, and you cannot find an identical replacement, you can change all the buttons for new ones. If a hole or permanent stain appears, due to moth damage or an accident, try repairing or patching it. Some dry cleaners offer an invisible mending service if you feel you are not up to repairing it yourself. Classic, good-quality clothes are worth preserving; fashion fads that might look ridiculous in a few years' time are probably not!

Storing

Before storing clothes, it is vital to make sure they are clean. If moths afflict your home—and they are a growing problem with the current fashion for buying secondhand or vintage clothing—dry cleaning is an effective, although not environmentally kind, solution. It will, however, kill the larvae that do the damage to clothes. The female moth lays her eggs on natural fabrics—cotton, wool, and silk. Moths are less fond of synthetic fibers. If the garment is clean, but you want to make sure that it will not become a larvae feast in storage, put it into the freezer for a couple of days, sealed in a plastic or wax paper bag—this kills not only moths but also their eggs.

Moth larvae enjoy human "soil" so it is essential that you store clean clothes only. Never store dry-cleaned clothes in the dry cleaner's plastic covering, as the residue of the chemicals in an airless space can turn the clothes inside yellow. There are many natural moth deterrents—the best are lavender, lemon peel, bay leaves, cinnamon, rosemary, and cedar wood. All of these will lose their efficacy after about a year, so must be replaced regularly. Clean the inside of the closet regularly and carefully. Vacuum the hidden dark corners where moth larvae might be lurking.

Lavender bags
These are wonderful gifts; and you can give new ones periodically to replace those that have lost their scent. Cut out large quantities of muslin squares, fill with dried lavender, and tie the tops with ribbon. Put them in pockets of clothing both in the closet and in storage to deter moths from setting up home.

Air and admire your clothes
If you have the inclination and a sturdy washing line in your garden, hang your clothes out to air on very cold, bright, and frosty days, turn out the pockets and brush each garment with a sturdy brush to get rid of any larvae or their parents. Moths dislike the cold and dislike bright light even more. Not only does this procedure deter moths, but a good brush and shake in the dry, cold air will make your clothes look and smell freshly cleaned.

Instead of washing or dry-cleaning cotton denim, try putting jeans in the freezer for a couple of days—this will make them smell fresh, disinfect them, and result in a longer life for the fabric.

LEFT: *Since babies grow so quickly and their sweet tiny socks have a very short useful life, reuse these little treasures by turning them into lavender bags.*

RIGHT: *Keep old cotton dresses and skirts beyond their useful life for transforming into patches, dustcloths, or smaller items of clothing.*

Caring for shoes

There are a few simple guidelines for looking after your shoes and boots so that they last you for years.

▶ Keep them clean and polished.

▶ Repair the soles and heels of shoes and boots as soon as possible to avoid permanent damage.

▶ Fill wet shoes and boots tightly with crumpled newspaper to keep them in shape, and leave them to dry naturally, then feed them with a really good natural polish.

▶ To remove odors from shoes, sprinkle baking soda inside them and leave for a couple of hours.

▶ Tennis shoes, my preferred choice of shoe for the entire summer, can be washed in the washing machine. Buy two or three pairs so that a clean pair is always available.

BELOW: *Like fine wine, classic washable tennis shoes improve with age!*

Laundering clothes

Wash cotton and other machine-washable clothes at low temperatures—the "warm" setting is perfectly adequate—with a cup full of baking soda (see page 30) added to the detergent powder (washing powder). This makes the powder much more effective and helps to extend the life of your washing machine. Add a cup of white distilled vinegar (see page 22) to the dispenser drawer instead of fabric conditioner to remove chemical residues and soften the fibers of the clothes.

When buying a new washing machine, check its green credentials and opt for the greenest appliance possible—they are not necessarily more expensive. If you have the option of an ecowash in the program, it will go some way to relieve your guilt when you follow my next instruction.

To keep beautiful, new, white underwear white, avoid washing it in too full a load. It is overfilling your machine that causes white underwear to turn gray. If your underwear is particularly precious, wash it by hand.

To treat stains, soak the item as soon as possible—fresh stains are much easier to deal with than dried stains—in a sink filled with a solution of baking soda and warm water. In an emergency, lemon juice is also a good stain remover, as it has bleaching properties. Rub half a lemon onto the stain, squeezing some of the juice directly onto it, then rinse with warm water. Never use hot water, as this can set the stain rather than remove it.

RIGHT: *To keep your whites white, simply avoid overloading the machine, rather than adding chemical whiteners to the wash.*

BELOW: *Soak stained fabric in baking soda to remove the blemish.*

IF YOU DISLIKE IRONING ...
Clothes sold as "non-iron" are treated with formaldehyde, so avoid buying them altogether—crumpled natural fabrics look better anyway.

Good drying methods

If possible, dry clothes outside in the fresh air. When the weather is inclement, air them inside on a wooden rack. This is always preferable to tumble drying, not only because it lessens carbon emissions but because your clothes will last longer if you avoid tumble-drying them.

A charming drying practice from long ago is to spread small items—pillowcases, underwear, baby clothes, and socks—on lavender bushes in the warm sun. The fibers will absorb the scent of lavender. This method is especially lovely for nightgowns and pillowcases—both adults' and children's—as the essential oil in lavender is known to promote restful sleep.

SMALL THINGS THAT CAN MAKE A BIG DIFFERENCE

▶ Investigate "wet clean" laundries to deal with your "dry clean only" items of clothing. They use a combination of steam, pure soap, and vacuuming to clean "dry clean only" clothes.

▶ Hand washing is always an eco-friendly option for dealing with small amounts of laundry.

▶ Instead of using bleach to whiten small cotton items, boil for a few minutes in a solution of water and lemon juice.

▶ Heating the water accounts for 90 percent of the energy used in washing machines—the "warm" setting is ample.

▶ Instead of using fabric softeners in your washing machine, which can leave chemical residue on your clothes, use white distilled vinegar to soften fabrics.

▶ If you want scented clothes and laundry, store lavender and herb bags, soap, and essential oils in the linen closet. The linens will absorb the fragrances into their fibers.

▶ Use powdered or tablet washing products in the washing machine and dishwasher. Liquid versions contain twice as many harmful chemicals.

LEFT: *Avoid using a tumble-dryer as much as possible, not only to reduce carbon emissions but also to make your fabrics last longer.*

RIGHT: *A plentiful supply of wooden clothespins and a sturdy length of washing line can save countless units of electricity, with the added bonus that clothes dried in the open air always seem to smell fresher.*

The linen closet

Just as for clothes, a good clear-out and straightening up of the linen closet does so much for morale, not to mention efficiency. As obvious as it may seem, you should divide the linen closet into well-labeled sections—it is something that will save much time and encourage those with access to the closet to keep it as neat as they found it.

To distinguish between twin, full-size, queen-size, and king-size bed linen, create a color-coded labeling system, using different colored ribbon or tape sewn onto each corner of the sheet. A single corner is never enough, because that will be the one neatly folded and hidden within the pile, and trying to get to it will cause chaos in the closet.

If you have inherited beautiful linens but find they are never used, tie them up in a pile with ribbon. This neat, orderly, and beautiful pile of linen will enhance the shelves; and even if the rest of the closet falls into disarray, the beribboned pile will give the appearance of a well-ordered household.

To keep the closet smelling sweet and free from moths (although these should not be a problem if the linens are regularly washed and hung out to air), slip lavender bags into the piles.

LEFT: *Store scented soap in the linen closet so that stacks of neatly folded sheets absorb a gentle aroma.*

RIGHT: *An orderly linen closet will bring much pleasure.*

CHAPTER 2

ENERGY FOR LIFE

In Europe and North America we still enjoy low-cost energy and an abundance of water, compared with many other parts of the world. As a result, we tend to squander these vital resources. We have huge reserves of cheap energy from prehistoric times, with vast areas of forest covering the land and enormous reserves of coal, oil, and gas, but all these gifts are finite, and all will, eventually, run out.

We depend (and I am not saying this is a bad thing) on other countries to provide much of our fuel. The bad part about this dependence is the possibility that one day we may find ourselves without the fuel to warm ourselves, to transport food, and to run our factories. A solution to this and other impending self-inflicted problems is to look back at the lives of our forefathers, who worked with nature and the natural world and had the expertise to be self-sufficient.

Water

Many parts of the world are experiencing dramatic, sometimes disastrous, extremes in the supply of water. In Britain, we normally have abundant rainfall, with infrequent summer droughts, but recently we've sometimes had too much of a good thing. The summer of 2007 brought almost tropical downpours to many parts of England, resulting in huge flood damage. About the same time, a persistent storm system in the American Midwest left huge areas of six states under water; twenty-seven counties were declared Federal Disaster Areas.

Much of this damage could have been averted by sensible planning: not building houses on flood plains; providing better surface water drainage. Warnings are now being voiced that replacing grass lawns with wooden decking and paved areas is another cause of flooding. Rainfall seeps into a lawn, but it remains on the surface of ground that is inappropriately clad.

BELOW: *Water is a precious resource upon which life depends. It should be treated with respect.*

The cost of fuel

Without doubt, energy costs will—and should—rise. The cost of energy has to reflect not just the supply and demand issue but also the environmental damage caused by different fuel sources. We are all in the same boat, because, whichever country our energy source is derived from, environmental damage is the same.

Energy is a resource imported and exported throughout the world—often from areas of political instability—and with no guarantee that it will continue to be available at a price we can afford, at a time when we need it, from a country that is willing to sell it to us. Emerging economies are energy hungry, and world reserves of hydrocarbon fuels are finite, with refining and distribution capacity struggling to meet demand—a demand that can only get worse. The question we should ask ourselves is why we are burning unrenewable fuels when we know the damage they do to the environment and when their sustainability is in doubt.

BELOW: *A well-kept woodland can produce power to heat homes in a sustainable way.*

Reducing energy in the home

The first thing for us to do is to reduce the energy used in the home. As individuals, we can take a number of steps that need not impact too dramatically on our comfort or ability to lead a satisfactory lifestyle.

Lifestyle changes

- Rise with the lark to make best use of the natural daylight.
- Travel by rail instead of by air, when possible, if necessary reworking your schedule to give yourself more time.
- Clean the windows and get used to using natural light instead of electric light.
- Wear more clothes when it is cold, rather than switching on the heating.
- Limit your use of air conditioning in the summer by planting shade-giving trees in appropriate positions to minimize strong sun getting into the house.

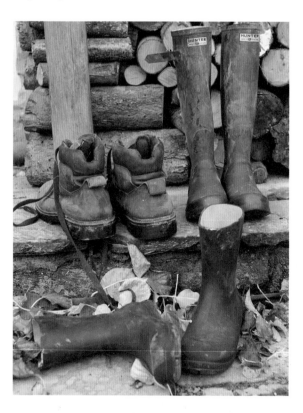

- Make a through draft by opening windows and doors that are opposite each other. You might consider making new window openings (make sure to obtain the necessary permits).
- If winters are cold where you live, you should be aware that wood floors absorb heat and keep it for longer than, for example, vinyl or tile floors. Properly insulated wooden floors absorb heat and keep it for longer. Make sure the boards are laid without gaps that would cause drafts.
- Get your house inspected by a qualified insulation advisor. You will receive advice on all aspects of energy saving, not to mention money saving.
- For extra protection from drafts, consider having your draperies interlined with table felt. The initial cost will be high, but the energy saving should pay for this in a short time.
- Place a brick or a filled bottle of water inside the toilet cistern. This will save at least 1 quart (one liter) of water every time you flush.
- Brush your teeth with the faucet (tap) turned off. Turn on only as necessary.

Household appliances

- Only buy appliances certified as energy efficient; look for the EnergyStar logo on the tag.
- There is no need to rinse dishes before putting them into the dishwasher—scrape remains into the garbage instead.
- Run the dishwasher or washing machine with full loads, as much as possible.

LEFT: *Boots made for walking—the very best form of green transportation!*

- Keep appliances running efficiently so that they use less electricity. Keep the heat exchanger at the back of the refrigerator dust free, and clean the inside of the dishwasher and washing machine with a solution of white distilled vinegar and baking soda.
- Defrost your freezer regularly.
- Avoid empty spaces in the freezer. Fill the empty parts of the freezer with bags of ice.
- If you're buying a new refrigerator, check its energy efficiency. As a general rule, models with the freezer on top or at the bottom are more energy-efficient than side-by-side models.
- Switch off unnecessary lights and use localized lamps instead of overhead lighting.
- Use low-energy lightbulbs. By changing all your normal light bulbs to compact fluorescent bulbs, you could save 75 percent of the energy you would have used.
- Install a timer on light switches, so that, when you are away, you don't need to leave lights on to deter burglars.
- Unplug chargers as soon as they have done their job. Up to 95 percent of energy used by chargers is wasted.
- Switch off appliances when not in use. It is not necessary to have the television, CD, and DVD players on standby. Resist the temptation to buy an exercise machine—there are many ways to burn calories that don't use electricity.

Kitchen practices
- Boil only as much water as you need.
- Chop vegetables smaller so that they cook more quickly, using less power.
- When reheating refrigerated items, first bring them to room temperature to reduce the amount of heat required.
- Always allow hot foods to cool down before placing them in the refrigerator.

RIGHT: *An alternative form of transportation, with no impact on the environment and beneficial for your health.*

Reducing our carbon footprint

There are now 7.6 billion people in this world. If we assume that just one-third of those people live in houses and all that one third of the population made these small changes to their lives, imagine how much energy those 2.5 billion people could save.

The greatest energy consumption per head is in our home and in our travel. Both these areas are within our control to moderate, and it need not cost us anything. Indeed it will save us all a great deal of money. By insulating our homes and using central heating only when absolutely necessary, and by investing in heat recovery systems and installing intelligent control systems and more efficient furnaces, we can do a huge amount to reduce our carbon footprint. Initially, these measures will cost money, but in the long run they will be less expensive than excessive oil or gas consumption, both to our pockets and, more importantly, to the environment.

RIGHT: *Avoid using chemical firelighters. A store of pinecones, dried lemon rinds, twigs, and tightly rolled newspaper is all you need to start a fire.*

BELOW: *Neatly stacked wood for fuel.*

Alternative energy sources

Once we have reduced our energy demand, we need to look at how to generate our reduced energy needs from fuels and sources that do not damage the environment. These should be sustainable and available—locally, where possible, to give us the security of supply.

For many, especially those who live in urban areas, the options for alternative fuels and energy sources for homes are more limited than for those who live in semi-rural and rural areas, purely because of space. However, there are systems tailor-made for individual properties and community schemes that are kind to the environment. Check the Web sites of energy providers to discover whether you are in a position to receive a greener power.

There are free sources of energy—as ever, kindly supplied by Mother Nature—but the harvesting of such energy often comes at a cost, both in monetary terms and in environmental impact.

In Europe, the energy used in homes produces more climate-changing greenhouse gases than the continent's entire manufacturing industry.

Wind farms and wind turbines

The capital cost of setting up wind farms is huge because the infrastructure required to connect them to the electric grid is costly. Some people also regard them as visually intrusive—personally, I find them exciting and beautiful. However, they work only when the wind blows, so we cannot yet depend on them entirely.

However, Britain is the windiest country in Europe with enough offshore wind to power the country three times over. According to Good Energy, Britain's only 100 percent renewable electricity supplier, we have the potential to power ourselves cleanly without relying on gas pipelines from other countries. In the United States, where wind power varies greatly from region to region, the picture is more complex; but technology enabling the networking of individual sites to equalize overall production is improving, and larger, more efficient turbines are being built.

For individuals, the options are to buy energy from a "green" supplier, or, subject to planning regulations, to install your own wind turbine (and solar panels—see right). Anything less than 6kW is probably only snipping at the edges of being economic. However, if you live in a very windy part of the world, the local utility will buy your wind power if you have a surplus.

LEFT: *If you burn wood, save the ash to use in the garden. Sprinkle it around plants to deter slugs from eating new shoots.*

Tidal power and hydropower

Although not a very convenient solution for inland populations, tidal power is another option. The tide is guaranteed, and the power systems using tidal power are known to work. However, the capital costs are enormous.

Hydropower has proved itself to be efficient, albeit with huge installation costs, and requires ugly pylons and cables. While the infrastructure could be buried underground, environmental damage might outweigh the benefits. However, it is another option for the experts to work on. Individual homes or communities can benefit from hydropower if there is access to a water resource of sufficient volume and flow. The installation of turbines in existing mills is a very real prospect, as the major engineering work has already been done. Smaller schemes relying on the head of water, rather than the volume, can take advantage of small, efficient generating plants.

Solar power

This power works well when the sun shines. Either direct solar heat or photo-voltaic cells generate electricity. The technology is getting better and less costly, and can work well for individual houses. Local government can help by revising planning codes to make them less restrictive on the installation of solar panels, and designers can help by improving their appearance. As part of a multi-technology installation, solar power can contribute all year round.

Biofuels

These fuels are produced from material that has been grown specifically for fuel production, or from material grown for other purposes that has generated a byproduct once called "waste." A recent criticism of the policy of taking vast acreages out of food production and diverting the crops to bioethanol and biodiesel production was that it potentially creates a shortage in world food supply.

This is a knee-jerk, selfish, and not very efficient policy to create road fuel. Worse still is the ripping up of rainforest to accommodate palm oil plantations. Both these practices are counterproductive and ecologically disastrous. As long as people are a priority in the agenda of those providing road fuel, the above solutions can be of real benefit, but when money is at the forefront of this progress, it is inevitable that the poor will suffer short term, and the rich in the long term.

RIGHT: *Electric lighting within the garden will increase your carbon footprint. Candles in jars are far more beautiful than even the cleverest outdoor lighting scheme.*

The future of energy supply

We can all help simply by reducing our dependence on cars. Governments can help by making public transportation more user friendly, cheaper, and more efficient.

There is scope for growing specific crops for energy, but only where there is no conflict with food production and environmental issues. Miscanthus (elephant grass) and short-rotation crops, such as shrub willow and poplar, are good examples of this.

To begin with, we need to focus on converting existing agricultural and forestry byproducts and waste to a fuel source that can be utilized to produce heat and, to a lesser extent, power. This can range from wood chip to straw and cereal wastes and processed wood waste. There is also the option of converting animal and human waste to generate electricity and heat.

Incineration of domestic and industrial waste—subject to careful control of incineration flue gases—is also a viable concept at an industrial scale, as well as on a smaller scale.

LEFT AND RIGHT: *A sustainable source of heating fuel.*

Forestry benefits

Increasing the area of land under forestry to produce sustainable wood for fuel would provide an endless resource. Planting and managing woodland also reduces carbon emissions because of the CO_2 absorbed and the oxygen given out by growing trees, and land is stabilized by the growing roots of trees.

More immediately, there is in tiny England in excess of 148,000 acres (60,000 hectares) of unmanaged woodland. If this huge acreage were managed carefully, it could produce wood fuel on a sustainable rotational basis. This would vastly improve the biodiversity of woodland, create employment in rural areas, and provide a source of income for woodland owners. More than 5.5 million tons (5 million tonnes) of wood waste is committed to landfill every year in Britain alone. In the United States, the figure is about 29 million tons (26 million tonnes); the cost of this disposal is reckoned to be about $1,124 annually.

Wood waste can be recycled in other ways besides fuel (for example, as wood chips for mulch); but its use as fuel is arguably the most important. Wood produces neglible amounts of sulfur—the substitution of wood for bituminous coal reduces sulfur emissions by 80 percent. And emissions of CO_2 are about 1 percent of those for burning oil. Industry is beginning to realize the economic value of this form of recycling. In the Southeast and Pacific Northwest, wood-related industries are supplying more than half of the energy they need by burning wood waste.

In Britain, which lacks the vast forest reserves of North America, nuclear fuel is advocated by some people as a "clean" option. But my opinion is that, until we know how to clean up the potential mess, we should not proceed.

CHAPTER 3

THE KITCHEN GARDEN

Growing your own fruit and vegetables has major
health benefits. Firstly, it forces you to take exercise in
the fresh air. The exertion needed for proper digging is
as close to aerobic exercise as I shall ever get; besides
we live in an area of extreme hills, so wheeling a
barrow full of waste must be equivalent to at
least an hour of walking on a treadmill.

Secondly, you benefit from knowing exactly
what your crops have been sprayed and fed with.
Another health benefit is the speedy transference
from the earth to your plate, which means that fruit
and vegetables retain more essential vitamins and
minerals. Eaten moments after picking, they taste so
much better than those transported halfway around
the world. Over time, sugars convert into starch, and
the longer the journey, the less sugar and more starch
food contains. The difference in the taste of homegrown or locally grown fruit and vegetables is like
the difference between a canned peach and one
freshly plucked from a tree.

Compost

Entire books have been written on the subject of composting, but as far as I am concerned, there are three reasons to compost. Firstly, my instinct, when confronted by a piece of fruit that shows evidence of occupation by slugs or other wildlife, is to throw it away; keeping a compost bin allows me to indulge my squeamishness with minimal waste. Knowing that it will rot to become a beautiful, black, loamy substance, which will improve the soil and encourage new growth in the garden, placates my conscience. Secondly, composting eases the load of waste collectors and therefore the quantity of landfill waste, and thus the release of carbon emissions from slowly rotting food. The third reason is the magical way that waste products become a valuable source of nutrients and improvers to the soil, giving back what has been taken from it.

"The soil is the gift of God to the Living."

Thomas Jefferson, 1813

BENEFITS OF COMPOSTING

▸ Compost enriches the soil by increasing the organic matter, so that plants are healthier and stronger.
▸ It provides natural, slow-release nutrients.
▸ Not only does compost help the soil to retain moisture; it also balances the pH levels.
▸ Compost reduces soil erosion.
▸ In winter, compost increases soil temperature, while in summer it lowers it, thus benefiting the plants.
▸ Sandy soils improve by gaining body, which will preserve moisture. Clay soils will gain a more open structure, so they drain better.

And all of this comes from what we consider to be waste material and would otherwise find itself in landfill. Good enough reasons, surely, for all of us with a garden, however large or small, to start composting with passionate commitment.

Kitchen compost bins

My kitchen compost bin is a vintage white enamel bucket. Probably 80 years old, it is still going strong. It is easy to clean and has a wholesome, traditional look about it.

I never cover my compost bucket while it is in the kitchen. The main reason is so that it does not get forgotten and begin its festering process inside the house. During the summer months, you may need to empty the kitchen compost bin daily as it tends to attract flies; in winter this is less of a problem.

LEFT: *My kitchen compost bin, recycling vegetable matter into wholesome compost for the garden.*

What to compost

Any raw vegetable matter that will rot down quickly is suitable for a compost heap. While decomposing, the compost heap will heat up, and the weeds should rot. However, it is a wise precaution never to put infected or diseased plants or weeds in seed into the compost heap. Put them on a bonfire instead, to make sure that the viruses are completely destroyed.

I incorporate flower water and the dregs from coffeepot and teapot for their moisture content. As with all house and garden matters, trial and error are key—what works for some might not work for others. However, a good result is unmistakable: a dark, even black soil with no hint as to what it has been made from. The following will all make good compost:

"40% of household waste can be composted at home, saving 20% of the UK's methane emissions from the slow decomposition of biodegradable landfill waste."

The Composting Association

- Vegetable peelings
- Vegetables and fruits way beyond their sell-by date
- Dead flowers, along with the old flower water
- Fallen petals and leaves
- Corrugated cardboard
- Egg boxes
- Coffee grounds
- Tea leaves and tea bags
- Eggshells (never whole eggs)
- Grass clippings
- Weeds (not in seed and also never bindweed)
- Torn-up newspaper
- Straw (essential)
- Fruit peelings—there is a debate about citrus fruit, but I put it in with no detrimental effect. (If you worry about putting citrus peelings into the compost heap, save lemon and orange shells, leave them to dry, and use them to light fires—see page 64.)

Never put cooked food (even vegetable waste) into the compost bin, as this attracts vermin.

ABOVE: Egg boxes can be added to the compost heap or used as containers for planting seeds.

Types of compost bin

Although I have survived with a single wooden bin that is built to resemble a beehive, in an ideal world you would make three compartments for your vegetable compost. One is for newly added waste, the second for shoveling the contents of the first compartment into, adding air and straw as you go in the turning process, and the third for storing the mature compost. If you have access to animal manure, the compost bin needs only two separate compartments. In one, turn the compost and allow it to mature; in the other, store the finished, mature compost before use.

Keep bins with processing compost covered to prevent saturation by rain and to keep in heat, which speeds up the rotting process. A piece of sisal matting or (not rubber-backed) natural pile carpet is suitable for this task.

Site the compost bins, which should ideally measure 4 feet (1.2m) square, in an area that is easy to access with a wheelbarrow, in a site where there is good air circulation, but out of the wind and away from fierce sun.

making compost

The main thing you need in making compost is patience, as it can take a long time for your household and garden waste to rot down into lovely, rich, crumbly earth. You can use a plastic urban bin, a two- or three-compartment wooden one, or just allocate a place in the garden to build a heap using no bin at all. Whatever you decide, air, moisture, and nitrogen are all essential ingredients for making good compost.

you will need

Plastic or wooden bin
(optional)
Straw
Garden waste
Household waste
Water
Activator
Garden fork

1 Stand the bin or build the heap on earth (not concrete or paving) so that worms can get in easily, and put down a layer of straw or twigs to allow air to circulate.

2 Add a layer of grass clippings and weeds, and if they are dry, sprinkle with water.

3 Then add the contents of your kitchen compost bucket, and keep adding suitable material, plus water when the heap gets too dry. Untreated cardboard tubes, such as empty paper towel rolls, help to add air.

4 Every week or so, turn the heap with a garden fork, and make sure the nitrogen content is boosted with activators to speed up the rotting process. Good natural activators include comfrey leaves, grass clippings, urine, and animal manure, if you have access to it (but not from cats or dogs). Otherwise, commercial activators are available.

Local government composting schemes

Some authorities have composting schemes whereby vegetable matter is delivered to a central store and compost is made from "donated" garden waste. However well meaning these schemes are, be aware that, unknowingly, some infected plants or annoyingly persistent weeds might lurk therein. Unless you are prepared to keep the compost for at least two years without using it, do not apply it to your garden. Many years of hard work could be ruined by the introduction of bindweed or potato blight. The best compost is your own compost, since you know exactly what it has been made from.

Poultry and farmyard manure

You can add fresh poultry, horse, and cow manure to the compost heap in small amounts, or apply well-rotted farmyard manure directly onto the ground. The solid part of the manure is rich in phosphates, while the urine contains nitrogen and potash, all of which are vital ingredients for healthy plant growth.

  If you do add fresh poultry manure, make sure that the birds have been reared organically. Poultry manure is richer than farmyard manure—six times richer in nitrogen and four times richer in phosphorus and potassium.

BELOW: *Manure that is acquired from happy, healthy poultry makes an excellent addition to the compost heap.*

Fresh poultry waste acts as an accelerator, speeding up the heating process within the vegetable compost heap. Organic poultry manure pellets can also be spread directly onto the ground—follow the instructions on the package.

Urban gardeners can buy organic manures—the Internet is a mine of information for supplies of organic gardening requirements. Investigate the source of the compost, if possible visiting the supplier. It is not unknown for some unscrupulous traders to claim their product is organic in order to charge much higher prices, when actually it is anything but.

Animal manure alone is an excellent fertilizer and soil improver, but it should be well rotted before use. However, you cannot always be sure as to the age of the manure, even if you are acquiring it from a local stable or farm. To avoid infecting your garden with weed seeds that have not completely rotted, I suggest you store the manure for at least a year or, better still, two years before use.

In the third century, the Romans encouraged their farm laborers to urinate into the compost heap. Today organic soil experts tell us that urine is still the best nitrogenous activator nature and humans can supply. I leave it to you to decide whether or how it should be added.

Spent mushroom compost
This improves the soil. Laid in a thick layer, it prevents weeds from growing and conserves heat and moisture. Suppliers can be found on the Internet.

Bracken and lamb's wool compost
Simon Bland and Jane Barker, hill farmers in England's Lake District, have created a compost using bracken and lamb's wool. Bracken is very high in nutrients, while wool has good water retention and is an excellent source of nitrogen. The recipe took six years to perfect, and it produces a soft, peatlike compost. However, unlike peat, the compost is made from waste products and does not have any damaging impact on the environment. For further information, visit their Web site: www.dalefootcomposts.co.uk.

ABOVE RIGHT: *Mushroom compost conserves both heat and moisture, and is an excellent soil improver.*

RIGHT: *Organically-reared sheep provide wool that, when added to compost, makes it rich in nitrogen.*

the kitchen garden **77**

Community gardens

If you don't have a large garden, see if there is a community garden in your area—ideally, the kind that offers plots for cultivation by individuals. Although you can use a courtyard, balcony, or roof terrace to grow at least some fresh fruit and vegetables—in pots, bins, old bathtubs and porcelain sinks—a plot of your own gives you more opportunity for diversity.

How community gardens work

A community garden can take various forms. Where I live, in Britain, the standard form is what we call an allotment garden. These are tracts of land owned by the local government and divided up into smaller plots, which are then leased to families or individuals, who use them to grow their own fruit and vegetables.

Allotment gardens go back more than 150 years. They were created to empower those on low incomes to improve the quality of their lives, their health and their diet by growing their own food. Allotments proved invaluable during the Second World War, and interest peaked as people responded to Britain's "Dig for Victory" demand for self-sufficiency. All town gardens, even those at Buckingham Palace, were turned into miniature farms. One and a half million plots on allotments were cultivated, and during this period 1.3 million tons of food were grown on 1.4 million plots every year.

Today, the allotment is still a cherished element of British life, providing nutritious fruit and vegetables for some 330,000 families. The local authorities charge a modest rental for each plot and they keep a close eye on how well they are maintained. In many areas there are long waiting lists for these gardens.

In other places, too, the value of community gardens is increasingly being recognized. Recent decades in the United States have seen a steady rise in their number—there are now more than 5,000. Some of these are allotment-style gardens; others are large single gardens cultivated collectively. In some cities, communal gardens occupy formerly vacant lots in downtown areas, and these gardens play a major role in fostering a strong community spirit.

Along with such social benefits, the health benefit of growing food free of harmful chemicals, and the ecological benefit of reducing food transportation, there is the sheer therapeutic value to be derived from gardening and from eating the fruits of one's labor. Information on

RIGHT: *Apples grown on a cordon take up little space on an small plot.*

community gardens (in Canada as well as the United States), as well as guidelines for starting and running them, can be obtained from the American Community Gardens Association (see their Web site: www.communitygarden.org).

A need for healthier lifestyles

In the West we are increasingly affluent; but in spite of this, the original need for community gardens as a means of improving the quality of life for those on low incomes remains. Startlingly, studies have revealed that poor nutrition still remains a problem within our cities, even though obesity is prevalent and a major concern in poorer communities.

This anxiety over our diet is acknowledged at government level, with increasing concern regarding obesity in the population. Public health campaigns are consistently emphasizing the importance of a diet high in fruit and vegetables, along with adequate exercise.

"Nearly two thirds of men and over half of women in England are now overweight or obese. And the problem here is increasing faster than in most other European countries. If prevalence continues to rise at the current rate, more than one in four adults will be obese by 2010. This would significantly increase the incidence of associated diseases, such as coronary heart disease, and would cost the economy over £3.5 billion [about $7 billion] a year by that date."

Sir John Bourne
Head of the National
Audit Office, *"Tackling
Obesity in England"*
February 2004

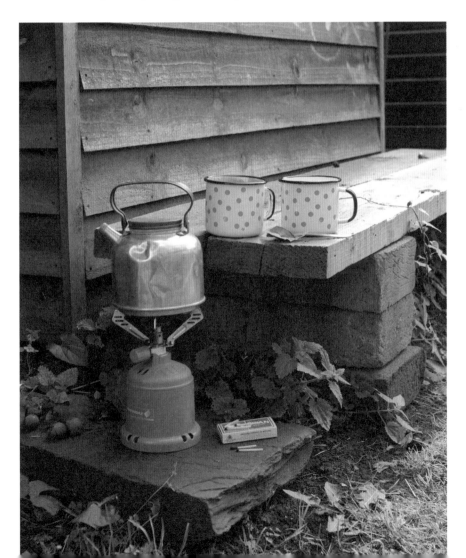

FAR LEFT (CLOCKWISE): *Lettuces past their best can be used to make good compost; a black sunflower grown to attract birds and bees (the seeds are both edible and easy to collect for next year's crop); strong and healthy rhubarb stems; strawberries growing in an old tin bathtub.*

LEFT: *Essential equipment for a British allotment: a gas burner for brewing tea, plus vintage enamel mugs.*

Green gardening

Although I cannot claim to know all that much about gardening, I have, after a fashion, managed to keep our small plot happy and healthy for the past 27 years. Trial and error is my method, backed up by tips and advice from proper gardeners—there is always something more to learn. We are self-sufficient (mostly) for at least three months of the year. When time allows, I will store crops efficiently and be more adventurous in my planting, and one day I shall have a greenhouse (the glass kind) where I can take cuttings, raise seeds, and be self-sufficient for at least six months of the year.

A basic guide to propagating

Most plants, especially those in the vegetable garden, will grow from seed. However, larger plants can be propagated by division or by cuttings. Layering, root cuttings, and grafting can also increase your plant inventory, but these three tasks require more knowledge than I have in order to explain them clearly. They are quite complicated and not guaranteed to work. If you really want to know how to perform them, buy a book dedicated to the subject. However, growing plants from seed is magical, growing from cuttings is fulfilling, and dividing established plants is hard work but nonetheless extremely gratifying.

Growing from seed

Growing from seed is the simplest and least expensive method of raising large numbers of plants.

The best time to sow most seeds is in the spring, for others the fall; however, successional planting throughout the seasons ensures a supply for longer. There are suggestions for dealing with the glut you will inevitably find yourself with in Chapter 4, "The Well-stocked Larder (pantry)" (see pages 122–143). All you need to know will be on the seed packet, unless you have been given seeds by a grower, in which case ask them for the sowing instructions. As a general rule of thumb, seeds should be sown at a depth equal to their thickness. I have yet to learn to pay proper attention to instructions and, more often than not, plant seeds too far apart or too close together. I am always surprised that plants really do grow from 8 in. (20cm) to 8 ft. (2m) within a growing season—so believe what you read!

Tender plants that will be affected by frost should be started in a coldframe or indoors in a greenhouse in late winter/early spring. In mid-spring sow hardy annuals directly into the ground where you want them to grow and flower. Herbaceous plants can be sown indoors in late winter or outdoors in late spring. Once you have made your planting plan and bought your seeds, there is nothing standing in your way to start growing all your own flowers and vegetables for the whole season ahead and, if stored carefully, into the winter too.

BELOW: Hand-thrown flowerpots—more ecologically sound than their plastic equivalents.

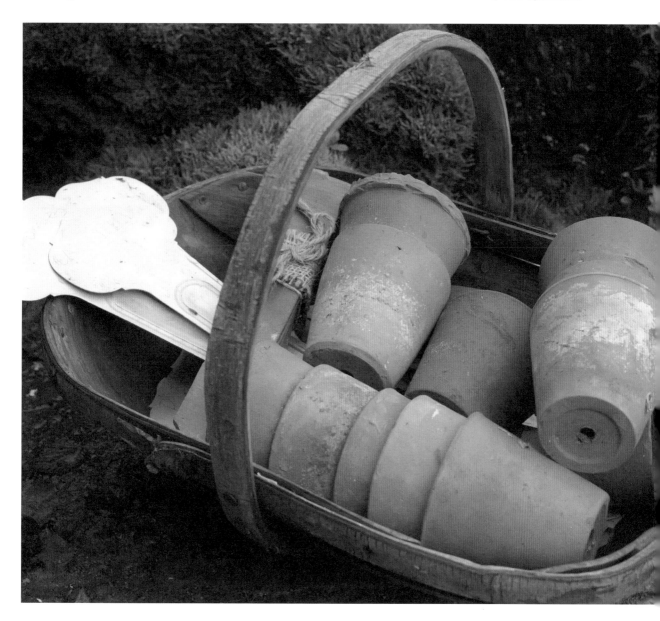

Materials and equipment

Without going into complicated detail—and it is not complicated—you will need the following for growing your own crops from seed:

1 Compost Make sure it is organic. Never buy peat, as this is an unsustainable product, which even though organic, is not ecologically friendly. Use a good commercial soil mixture designed for seedlings, with a loose, crumbly texture, consisting mainly of sterilized loam and sand (not homemade compost, which is hard to sterilize).

2 Seed tray or small pots An egg tray is a very eco-friendly container for small seedlings, allowing them to be planted directly into the soil in their biodegradable pots without disturbing the tiny root systems. Similarly, you can make your own pots with newspaper (see page 86).

   If you are reusing an old seed tray or pot, make sure it is clean and does not carry old viruses or molds from previous planting or old age. To disinfect it, wash with a solution of one part warm water and one part distilled white vinegar.

3 Watering can with rose head

LEFT: *Seedlings started in empty cardboard egg boxes can be planted straight into the ground, which helps keep their fragile roots intact.*

Planting seeds

Fill the container with compost, lightly firming with your hand, or shake gently to distribute the soil evenly. Following directions on the seed packet, sow large seeds in rows, or scatter finer seeds on the surface of the soil. Cover with a thin layer of compost. When sowing fine seeds, it is sometimes easier to control where they fall, and to distribute them more evenly, if you mix them with a small amount of sand before sowing.

ABOVE: *Young seedlings, planted in plugs.*

LEFT: *Pots placed on top of sticks protect gardeners from wounding themselves on the sticks and also confuse birds and other creatures, thus protecting the emerging pea crop.*

newspaper plant pots

For providing a feelgood factor, these planters are ideal. They are not difficult to make, are excellent for raising your own plants from seed, and take all the effort out of the job of planting out. If you don't have a suitable jar on hand, you can use a rolling pin.

you will need

Newspaper

Scissors

Straight jar or rolling pin

Damp soil mix

Seeds

Wooden seed tray or plate

1 Cut or tear newspaper into pieces measuring 8 x 5 in. (20 x 13cm).

2 Wrap a couple of pieces tightly around a straight jar, leaving a 2-in. (5cm) overlap at the bottom.

3 Fold the excess newspaper in across the bottom of the jar and stamp it on a hard surface to settle the newspaper in place.

4 Carefully pull the jar out of the newspaper mold and fold the top inward to help keep the pot straight.

5 Fill with slightly damp soil mix, and push the seeds into the soil. Prepare several pots, and stand them on a rigid surface, such as a wooden seed tray or a plate, and keep the soil moist until the seedlings emerge. Then plant out the newspaper pots intact.

Which crops to grow from seed

Depending on where you live, there are thousands of different vegetables in just as many varieties. I suggest you experiment—you will soon find out what suits your soil, your climate, and your patience. To avoid gluts of the same foods, sow as wide a variety as possible, and try to plant crops that can be harvested at different times of the year. It is also wise to choose those vegetables and fruits that are expensive to buy, as well as, of course, the ones that you are particularly fond of.

The following can be grown from seed in the garden or in pots on your balcony or windowsill:

Vegetables:
artichokes
asparagus
beets (beetroot)
bell peppers
borlotti beans
broccoli
brussels sprouts
cabbages
carrots
cauliflower
celeriac
celery
cucumbers
eggplants (aubergine)
fava beans (broad beans)
fennel
garlic

green beans
green onions
Jerusalem artichokes
kale
kohlrabi
leeks
lettuce
onions
parsnips
peas
pole lima beans
potatoes
pumpkins
radishes
rutabagas (swedes)
scarlet-runner beans
shallots
sprouting broccoli

squash
sweet potatoes
sweetcorn
tomatoes
turnips
vegetable marrows
zucchini

Fruit:
blueberries
grapes
raspberries
red currants
rhubarb
strawberries
white currants

BELOW: *A good crop of peppers can be raised in purchased "grow bags" as they require little space.*

BELOW LEFT: *A fine eggplant, successfully grown in a pot.*

BOTTOM: *The beautiful veined leaves of a common cabbage—perfect leaves with absolutely no help from pesticides.*

Flowering plants from seed

The variety of flowers that you can grow is limited only by your imagination. The three species of flowers that I grow abundantly in my garden are roses, sweet peas and lavender. These are generous in their provision of cut flowers, simple to grow and undemanding in their need for attention. Although we are often given plants and seedlings by friends and neighbours, I still enjoy the thrill of buying unusual varieties from local nurseries.

Enormous garden centers are popping up all over the place, but I find them soulless, homogenized, and uninspiring, with rank upon rank of identical perfect plants, imported mostly from abroad. Again, as with most of what is available to buy, it is better by far to support local growers—partly because the indigenous species they grow will thrive, but mainly because they are a dying breed; as long as there are huge supermarket-like nurseries cornering the market, supplying cheap but ordinary alternatives, their livelihoods and expert knowledge are in danger of disappearing.

TOP LEFT: *At the end of the flowering season, collect seed heads for drying. The bunches can be hung upside down, with the heads enclosed in a paper bag to collect the seeds as they drop. Alternatively, gently shake the seed heads inside a paper bag. Store the seeds in clearly labeled envelopes, ready for planting next season.*

RIGHT: *Throughout the season, keep cutting sweetpea flowers to prevent seed heads from forming and using up valuable energy. One packet of seeds can keep the house in flowers for the whole summer.*

BOTTOM LEFT: *Sunflowers attract wildlife, which consume unwanted pests.*

Growing from cuttings

So much money can be saved if you propagate your own plants by taking cuttings. It is terribly easy and most gratifying. If you have no garden, invest time in taking cuttings that can grow on your windowsill. Swap your time and effort for garden space with someone who can grow on your cuttings and provide you with the fruits of your joint labor.

The best time to take cuttings is in spring or summer, when plants have new, vigorous, leafy growth. There are a variety of ways to propagate from cuttings, each with its own requirements. As a general rule, cuttings need adequate light, warmth, and moisture. Avoid taking very small cuttings because they tend to exhaust their food reserves before their roots are formed.

A free-draining rooting medium capable of retaining sufficient moisture will encourage the cuttings to form roots. Buy good-quality medium because using a sterilized medium prevents diseases from being passed on to vulnerable new plants.

Taking root

Some plants root easily if the cuttings are placed in water. Basil stems placed in a vase of water grow roots quickly, and the rooted cuttings can then be planted to create a good basil crop. Rooting hormone is very helpful when taking cuttings, because the organic compounds hasten the formation of roots, creating sturdier plants in a shorter time.

Woody-stemmed plants, such as lavender, box, mock orange, and geraniums, are ideal sources of cuttings. All of these plants have the added benefit of creating a striking display when planted in quantity, such as box hedges surrounding beds, and whole borders of lavender.

ABOVE: *All the box plants in my garden are descended from three plants bought a quarter of a century ago.*

LEFT: *Plants grown from cuttings in abundance.*

taking cuttings

If you have a propagator, so much the better, but a deep seed tray is perfectly adequate. Line it with newspaper, then fill it with soil.

You will need

Plant from which to take cuttings
Rooting hormone
Old saucer
Newspaper
Cuttings tray

1 Cut the stem of a nonflowering shoot just below the place where the leaf is sprouting.

2 Remove the lowest leaves on the cut stem.

3 Pour some rooting hormone into an old saucer, and dip the base of the cutting first in water, then in the powder, making sure it is well coated.

4 Fill the cuttings tray with rooting medium, and smooth it over. Push the cutting into the soil and gently firm the earth around it. Plant several cuttings of the same species in the same cuttings tray, keeping them apart from each other. When they are tall enough to handle, plant them out either in the garden or in larger containers.

Seasonal guide to growing your own produce

This seasonal list will help you plan your garden month by month. In addition to helpful advice on vegetables, there is information on growing fruits and flowers.

Spring

▶ Keep digging to prepare the soil, applying compost and manure and a good sprinkling of Epsom salts (see page 105).

▶ Start successional sowing of salad crops.

▶ Cover emerging shoots with muslin or burlap when there is danger of frost.

▶ Protect young cucumber shoots from cucumber beetles by covering with cheesecloth until they start to flower.

▶ Sort out your seeds into months for sowing.

▶ Sow fava beans (broad beans) outside—the earlier they are sown the hardier they will be and less likely to be attacked by blackfly.

▶ Plant carrot and any other seeds suitable for early sowing, following instructions on the packets.

▶ Sow flower seeds, planting enough to supply the house with cut flowers and enough to give as gifts.

▶ Divide plants in the border to increase your stock and make more space.

▶ Organize plant swaps with friends and neighbors, so that you can give away a surplus of particular plants and receive others that you lack.

▶ Where necessary, support plants with bamboo sticks firmly pushed into the ground. Do this before the plants start toppling over, so that you are less likely to damage roots while inserting the sticks and can encourage plant growth in the right direction from the start.

▶ Regularly hoe between rows to keep the soil free of weeds.

▶ Earth up potatoes to encourage a good crop.

ABOVE: *Freshly pulled bunches of carrots— their sweet flavor is unlike anything bought from the supermarket.*

RIGHT: *If properly looked after, old garden tools will last many lifetimes.*

Summer

▶ Continue successional sowings of flowers and vegetables.

▶ Plant out tender vegetables and plants as soon as risk of frost has passed.

▶ Plan time off, so that you can make full use of your crops when they are ready to be frozen or made into pies, jams, jellies, and relishes.

▶ Regularly deadhead roses to encourage flowering.

▶ Watch out for aphids, blackfly, and other pests. On healthy, strong plants, use a hose to wash them off or wipe them off with a gloved hand.

▶ Encourage predators, such as ladybugs and hover flies (syrphid flies), by companion planting. (This involves growing pollen-rich flowering plants close to vegetable plants to attract beneficial insects. Marigolds smell bad to aphids and attract hover flies, which feed on aphids. Companion plants can also be used to entice destructive pests away from crops. For example, nasturtiums are easy to grow from seed and are a popular companion plant to cabbages and lettuces because they attract caterpillars.) Pesticides made from insecticidal soap or canola oil are also available.

▶ To rid plants of aphids and blackfly, boil torn-up rhubarb leaves in an old saucepan set aside for the purpose, and use the liquid to spray affected plants. This insecticide contains oxalic acid, which is poisonous to aphids and to man, so spray only onto nonedible plants, as a last resort.

▶ In late summer, harvest crops such as onions and shallots, leaving them to dry in the sun.

▶ Plan the storage and use of crops. Make sure you have the ingredients and the wherewithal to pot jams and jellies, chutneys, and other relishes.

▶ Cut herbs and dry them to ensure a stock throughout the winter.

LEFT: *Onions need to be perfectly dry before storing.*

- Continue to feed and weed the soil, and continue planting throughout the season.
- Dig up perennial weeds, such as dandelions and docks, completely removing the roots from the soil. A three-year-old dandelion left to seed will produce around 5,000 weeds. A stitch in time …
- At first sight of bindweed, dig gently down to its root, remove carefully, and destroy. This weed has the ability to set down roots from just a tiny piece of carelessly left stem. Vigilance and instant removal are the only organic method for keeping your garden clear of this virulent weed. Never put bindweed on the compost heap—put it on a bonfire.
- Spraying neat vinegar onto weeds growing in difficult-to-access places will get rid of them permanently.
- Remember to stop and savor the beauty of your garden.

LEFT: *To kill weeds that are difficult to remove between cracks in paving, treat with neat vinegar.*

Fall

▶ Lift and store vegetables before the first frosts arrive.
▶ Tidy fallen leaves and other debris, collecting sticks and pine cones for use as fire lighters.
▶ Continue with the harvest, preserving and freezing produce.
▶ Cut and freeze or dry herbs for use during the winter.
▶ Plant winter salad crops in pots to grow on the windowsill.
▶ Check your apples in storage, and remove any that are showing signs of deterioration immediately.

Winter

▶ On fine, mild days, begin digging the border and the vegetable patch.
▶ Check stored vegetables and fruit, and remove any that are not healthy.
▶ Protect tender plants with muslin or burlap.
▶ Prune fruit trees and roses.
▶ Plant bare-rooted shrubs and trees.
▶ Check your apples in storage, and immediately remove any that are showing signs of deterioration.
▶ Send for seed catalogs and plan your planting.
▶ You can continue to harvest winter crops such as rutabagas, parsnips, brussels sprouts, leeks, and cabbages.

BELOW: *Red and green lettuces planted together for dramatic effect.*

- Keep turning your compost heap.
- If you have bought a Christmas tree growing in a pot, it's a good idea to repot it into a larger pot and feed it. Then leave it outside until next Christmas.
- Winter is a good time to clean and sort out the potting shed, if you have one, and prepare pots and seed trays. Disinfect them with a solution of distilled white vinegar and warm water.
- Clean tools and wipe them down with a rag dipped in olive oil.
- Sharpen cutting tools and then wipe with an olive-oil rag.
- Clean and disinfect the greenhouse using nontoxic substances, such as distilled white vinegar or borax substitute.

BELOW: *A variety of plants, grown from cuttings, are sheltered by the side of a garden shed.*

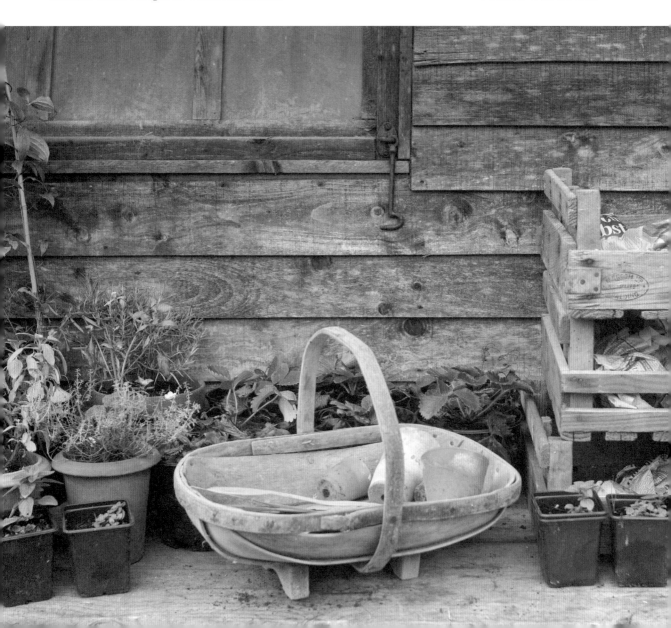

Water

Without it we can't eat; with too much of it, we can't eat. Last year, in England, we suffered from drought; this year we were inundated with flash floods. So it is hard to know exactly what will become of the weather. Until recently we were "threatened" with Mediterranean summers, and it was supposed that we would have to replace turnips with olive trees; the reality this year was very different. I think we have learned our lesson—not to believe anyone's predictions about the weather. No one really knows the extent of the damage we have done to our Earth's atmosphere and the effects that we will have to learn to live with, so practically we should prepare ourselves for all eventualities. I am writing this chapter in autumn and have just seen a branch of one of my apple trees in blossom—if trees think it is spring, imagine how confused I am! I also know of a hawthorn tree that is so confused it is bearing blossom, berries, and new leaf, as well as old, all at the same time. Nature's confusion should be considered as a gentle warning to us.

Lawns and flower beds

Before the onset of "decking mania," heavy rain was accommodated by lawns and flower beds. Now the water just runs off into drains, and heavy downpours, combined with thousands of decked gardens, result in huge quantities of water overwhelming the drainage systems.

Lesson number one: reinstate your lawn and your flower beds to slow down the water runoff. It is true that cutting the lawn is one less job when the whole garden is covered in decking, but tending a lawn—keeping it perfectly groomed and weed free—can become a bit of a healthy obsession. Flower beds might seem hard work compared to pots, but, on the whole, looking after a small flower bed is less work than looking after pots. For one thing, when it does rain, there are deeper reserves in the soil than there are in pots, and there is so much more choice in planting a flower bed. From flowers for cutting to vegetables and fruit, there is so much more scope to be self-sufficient with a flower bed.

RIGHT: *Using a watering can instead of a hose makes us more aware of how valuable each drop of water is.*

Collecting rainwater

If we assume there will be water shortage, it makes sense to accept the gifts provided by the heavens and conserve rainwater. Depending on where you live—whether or not mosquitoes are a serious problem in your area—you may be able to store rainwater in a barrel or storage tank. But first check your local building codes to make sure this is legally permissible. If it is, make sure to position the tank away from areas where you eat or sunbathe. However, there are more decorative options, such as a garden pool or even a little waterfall or fountain (the small pumps required use little electricity). Any flies or mosquitoes should be kept in check by dragonflies, and with clever planting around a pool, you can encourage other predators, such as frogs, to take up residence.

Making the most of water

It is important to water plants efficiently, and there is much that can be done to preserve and protect plants during periods of drought.

▶ Make sure your soil's structure is as good as it can be, with adequate additions of organic compost to all soils, and sand to heavy clay soils.

▶ Install a water barrel to collect rainwater (if permissible in your area), and make sure your gutters are clear of leaves and other debris for good flow.

▶ Mulch plants with a good layer of wood or bark chips, which not only conserves moisture but suppresses weeds.

▶ Keep flower beds free from weeds, which compete with your plants for nutrients and water reserves.

▶ Water with a watering can, and pour the water directly onto the roots. Don't overfill the can, making it heavy to carry, because the water is easily spilt.

▶ Always water during the early morning or in the evening, when your efforts won't be wasted by the drying effects of the sun.

▶ Choose plants that are suited to your environment—it makes life so much less complicated.

▶ Use water-retaining granules, which conserve water and release it slowly.

▶ Investigate replumbing your home to make good use of "gray" water. Bathwater and dishwashing water that does not contain any toxic chemicals can be used to water plants. This method of watering is best kept for flowering plants, rather than food plants.

▶ Invest in a clever invention: "WaterGreen," a simple gadget invented by Louise Angus and Antonia Lord (see page 187). A simple hand-squeeze pump, it turns a hose into a siphon that drains bathwater effortlessly through the hose, to any place that is lower than the bath. As long as only natural unguents and bath preparations are used, the "gray" bathwater can be redirected to the garden below.

RIGHT: *Water roses at their roots in the early morning or at dusk so that water does not evaporate, and to ensure a continuous supply of blooms.*

Feeding plants and shrubs

Along with homemade organic compost, a major, but little-known asset to the gardener's store cupboard is a good supply of Epsom salts. Their beautifying and health-giving properties are listed in Chapter Five (see page 167), but the benefits of this completely natural compound to the garden are also numerous—I cannot recommend Epsom salts highly enough. A generation ago, they were frequently used in the garden and in the medicine cabinet, but Epsom salts seem to have fallen by the wayside in recent years, replaced by more "up-to-date" chemical formulas, many of which cause more harm to the garden than good.

Studies have shown that magnesium and sulfur (two of the components of Epsom salts), enrich the soil to benefit vegetable crops and flowering plants.

The benefits of using Epsom salts include

- helping seeds to germinate
- promoting bushier plant growth
- encouraging flowering plants to produce more flowers
- increasing chlorophyll production in plants
- improving the phosphorus and nitrogen uptake of plants.

LEFT: *Container gardening on a grand scale—feed pots regularly and remove dead flower heads to keep the display healthy and ensure continuous flowering.*

How Epsom salts work

Crop research has found that magnesium is a vital mineral for seed germination and helps plants to produce chlorophyll, which transforms sunlight into food. Magnesium also helps plants to absorb phosphorus and nitrogen, two major fertilizer components. Sulfur is also an important plant nutrient, promoting chlorophyll production.

Although magnesium and sulfur occur naturally in the soil, they can be depleted by factors such as excessive rainfall and heavy agricultural use. Unlike most commercial fertilizers, which build up in the soil over time, Epsom salts are not persistent, so can't be overused. Tests by Britain's National Gardening Association show that roses fertilized with Epsom salts are much healthier, grow much bushier, and produce more flowers than those treated with commercial fertilizer.

Epsom salts can be used to encourage leaf growth on fruit and vegetables, such as tomatoes, lettuce, broccoli, cauliflower, cabbages, and other brassicas, and to promote leaf growth and plentiful flowers on shrubs, flowering plants, and fruit trees. Apply the salts every 4–6 weeks throughout the growing season from spring until early fall.

Dissolve four handfuls into 2½ gallons (about 10 liters) of water—this quantity will drench a 50-square-foot (about 15 square meters) plot. Alternatively, sprinkle around the roots of plants and water in.

When planting new rose trees and bushes, sprinkle a handful into the newly dug hole before planting. Apart from compost and manure, the only substance I use to encourage growth in my garden is Epsom salts.

ABOVE: *At Cabbages & Roses, we package Epsom salts in cans made from ecologically sound metals.*

BELOW: *Use water in which eggs have been boiled to water plants—this will give them much-appreciated calcium.*

ACID-LOVING PLANTS

To water acid-loving plants, such as azaleas, mix one cup of vinegar to 1 gallon (about 4.5 liters) of water. Immerse plants in buckets containing this solution until the water stops bubbling.

comfrey fertilizer

Comfrey leaves contain allantoin, an agent that stimulates healthy tissue formation. For this reason comfrey is used in medical treatments and beauty preparations. The leaves can also be used to make a very effective natural fertilizer. Grow a patch in the garden for a continuous supply.

you will need
Comfrey leaves
Enamel bucket
Heavy stone
Water
Funnel
Bottle

1 Collect enough leaves to layer nearly to the top of an enamel bucket, and place a heavy stone on top of them.

2 Add 1 pint (450ml) of water, and leave to rot in a warm place for about a month.

3 Drain the liquid from the bucket, and store in a clean, labeled bottle. Using a funnel makes it easier.

4 To use, make a solution of one part comfrey liquid to four parts water, and feed it to growing plants of all kinds.

Garden pests

The battle against pests in the garden is never ending, which makes it very tempting to resort to toxic chemicals. However, as well as being unkind—I hate the thought of even a slug dying a slow and painful death—toxic substances are not really necessary, because there are other methods that are just as effective.

Organic farmers control both disease and pests by clever planting (see pages 114–115) and by encouraging the wildlife species that are the natural predators of the pests that we spend so much time, money, and greenhouse gases trying to eliminate. Nature has a balance and, if left to her own devices, will manage to feed wildlife and mankind, so long as we show her the respect she deserves.

Natural pest control

All the natural methods of pest control that follow are as adequate as their chemical counterparts. Unlike commercial pesticides, they do not harm the natural predators of pests or the environment.

One of the most effective ways to prevent infestation is to grow strong, healthy plants. In my experience, these can survive an occasional attack from small pests if you are vigilant and react quickly.

Slugs and snails

Humane snail and slug traps Make humane traps for snails and slugs by burying bowls of beer in the soil, pouring in enough beer to drown a decent-sized slug. The enticing odor of the beer will attract the pests so that they slither into the bowl, get drunk, and drown. Milk and water is an alternative lure, but I prefer the idea of a drunk slug drowning to the rather sweet idea of a slug with milk whiskers. Humane traps are an infinitely kinder method of ridding the garden of one of its most irritating pests than using toxic slug pellets, which are eaten by slugs, and the slugs in turn are eaten by birds.

Remember to empty the traps often and renew the beer; this is not a pleasant task but is infinitely preferable to the disappointment of watching all your hard work in the garden disappear in a slime trail.

RIGHT: *Avoid slug damage to hostas by planting in a pot, rather than in the ground. Apply a thick layer of petroleum jelly around the top of the pot to prevent slugs from entering.*

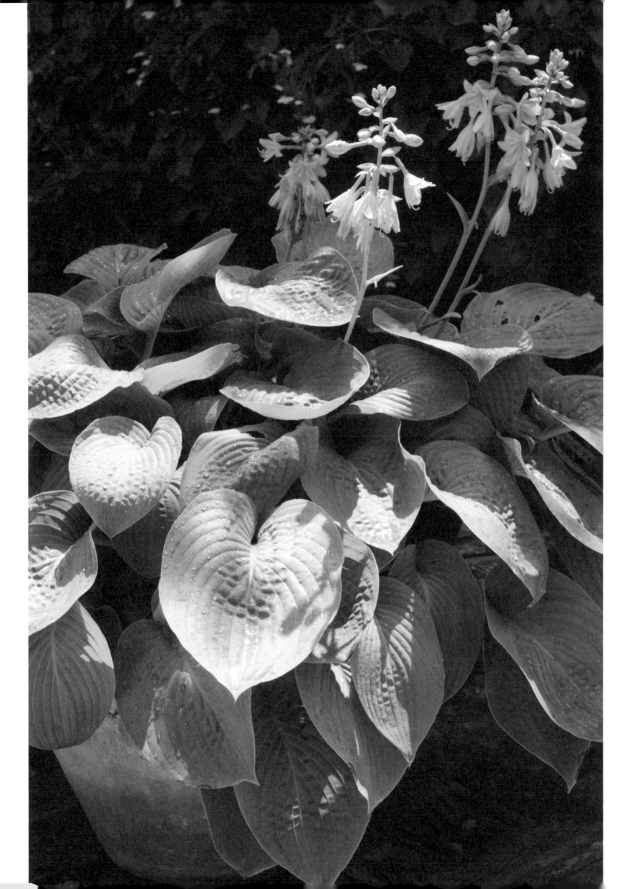

Snail and slug deterrents Snails and slugs dislike slithering over sharp, gritty materials, so put layers of wood ash around tender emerging plants, especially hostas, which are favored by slugs. Renew after rainfall.

Sharp Christmas tree branches laid around seedlings will protect plants for a while. However, the branches need to be renewed, as rainfall softens the ground and buries the needles. Dry, crushed eggshells have the same effect.

To prevent snails and slugs from climbing up pots to eat your plants, apply a thick layer of petroleum jelly around the pot about 1 in. (2.5cm) from the top. This method can also be used around holes in tree bark. Copper tape also deters the creatures from getting near your seedlings.

Slug-eating wildlife Encourage wildlife, such as birds and frogs, which will feast on slugs. Whatever you do, don't use lethal slug pellets, as these are also lethal to the slugs' and snails' natural predators. Harmless garden snakes, such as garter and milk snakes, should be allowed to go about their business—which includes preying on your resident gastropods. Learn to identify these useful reptiles and make them welcome.

BELOW: *Rhubarb—for eating and for pest control.*

Weeding

Weeds can encourage disease in plants of the same species—for example, shepherd's purse and charlock are members of the brassica family. If they are harboring clubroot, this can be passed on to your cabbage crop.

Barriers

In many cases, a barrier of some kind will protect your plants adequately from pests. A floating row cover, made of porous polypropylene sheeting, spread tent-fashion over your seedlings and weighted at the edges with stones, will protect them from harmful insects. Fruit trees benefit from being covered with netting. If birds are denied the opportunity to feast on your fruits, they are more likely to opt for an alternative diet of slugs and flies.

More vigorous invaders, such as rabbits, deer, or raccoons, require more substantial barriers. Rabbits may be put off by dense, thorny shrubs. For deer, a stout wire fence, 6 ft. (2m) or more in height, will be effective—although you may prefer to discourage them by planting species that they find repellent, of which there are many. Raccoons are more determined; and they are such a menace in some American states that it's legal to hunt them. Far kinder is the use of a humane trap, from which the animal can be released into the wild.

Protecting fruit trees

Tie corrugated cardboard around the trunks of fruit trees in late summer.
It will provide a home for a variety of fruit-tree pests, such as moth grubs
and weevils. Remove the cardboard after a week or two and destroy it; start
again with new cardboard.

Crop rotation

To keep soil healthy, crop rotation is an essential part of organic gardening.
This is because each crop tends to leach the soil of a particular nutrient.
Planting the same crop over and over again will exhaust the soil of that
nutrient. Crop rotation allows the nutrient balance to become reestablished,
and prevents pests and diseases particular to specific crops from building up
in the soil. Never plant the same crop in the same bed for two years
running. Keep planting plans from year to year, because it is very easy to
forget which plant has been grown in which bed.

BELOW: *A homemade cage, created from recycled wood and wire mesh, protects a crop from pests.*

Attracting beneficial insects

Some companion plants (see pages 114–115) not only deter particular crop pests but also attract the insects that feed on them. Planting specific shrubs to attract butterflies, hover flies, and bees adds to the beauty of the garden; and, by encouraging the right kind of wildlife, you are dealing with the wrong—damaging—kind. Shrubs require little effort, and some are also generous in providing cut flowers for the house.

SHRUBS FOR WELCOMING WILDLIFE

Butterfly bush (*Buddleia davidii*) Lavender (*Lavandula*)
English ivy (*Hedera helix*) Lilac (*Syringa* x *hyacinthiflora*)
Escallonia Privet (*Ligustrum quihoui*)
Heather (*Calluna vulgaris*) Blackberry (*Rubus*)
Firethorn (*Pyracantha*) Sage (*Salvia officinalis*)
Hebe (*Hebe albicans*) Thyme (*Thymus vulgaris*)

Bees: the gardener's friend

It is thought that there are 30,000 different species of bees in the world, and one-third of our food supplies depends on pollination by bees and other insects. Encourage bees to visit your garden by planting blue, white, yellow, and purple flowers for their ultraviolet properties.

Honey from bees living in or near towns is far more delicious than honey from hives in farmland. This is because of the variety of flowers producing the nectar that flavors honey; acres of the same crop create no variety.

Ladybugs

Encourage ladybugs into your garden for they eat aphids and blackfly. Ladybugs like to lay eggs in nettles, so leaving a small nettle patch to flourish in your garden should increase ladybug numbers. One ladybug that lives for one year can eat more than 5,000 aphids. If a plant is infested with aphids, don't panic and spray it with a chemical pesticide—once ladybugs reach that plant, they will eat the aphids quickly. If there is no sign of ladybugs dealing with the problem, spray with a strong jet of water from a hose to wash the aphids off.

RIGHT: *Lavender thrives in dry, sunny spots and will encourage wildlife into the garden.*

TIPS FOR OTHER GARDEN PESTS AND DISEASES

Powdery mildew
To prevent powdery mildew on grapes, spray with a mixture of 1 teaspoon of baking soda (bicarbonate of soda) and ½ teaspoon liquid soap in a gallon of water. Avoid applying this in full sun.

Blackfly and aphids
If your strong, healthy plants are infested with blackfly or aphids, wash off the pests instead of killing them with pesticides. Spray water directly from a hose without a fitting on the end, putting your finger on the hose outlet to control the strength of the water jet.

Moles
To deter moles from digging holes in your garden leaving unsightly, although useful, crumbly earth, bury plastic bottles in the ground, leaving about 1 in. (2.5cm) of the bottle neck exposed. The noise from the wind blowing across the top of the bottle neck will deter the moles. You can use glass bottles, but I feel this might be dangerous if you should forget about them being there and mow them accidentally.

Protecting seeds
Prevent the seeds of peas and beans planted outside from being eaten by birds, mice, or rabbits by covering them with chicken wire secured by pegs.

BELOW LEFT: *Ladybugs are one of nature's best defenses against aphids.*

BELOW: *Nettles growing wild are a good source of nutrients for both humans and plants, and they encourage ladybugs.*

Companion planting

This is a time-tested method of deterring pests without the use of chemicals. Frequently it is the aromatic foliage or flowers of the companion plant that either deter the pest or entice it away from the main crop plants—effectively acting as a decoy.

VEGETABLE/FRUIT	PLANT NEXT TO OR NEAR:
asparagus	basil, parsley
cabbages	beets (beetroot), celery, chamomile, and other herbs, onions, rhubarb
carrots	lettuces, marigolds, onions, tomatoes
celery	cabbages, onions, nasturtiums, tomatoes

BELOW: *My vegetable patch—all the box hedging has been grown from cuttings from three plants bought 25 years ago.*

VEGETABLE/FRUIT	PLANT NEXT TO OR NEAR:
corn	cucumbers, fava beans, potatoes, beans, peas, radishes, sunflowers
cucumbers	fava beans, marigolds
eggplants (aubergines)	celery, cucumbers, strawberries
fava beans (broad beans)	radishes, strawberries
lettuce and salad crops	cabbage, carrots, lettuce
onions	beans, carrots, corn, cucumbers
peas	cabbages, corn, marigolds
potatoes	corn, marigolds
pumpkins	cucumbers, lettuce, peas, nasturtiums
radishes	corn, radishes
scarlet runner beans	cauliflowers, celery, strawberries
spinach	corn, marigolds
squash	fava beans, lettuces, onions, spinach
strawberries	asparagus, carrots, marigolds, parsley
tomatoes	

HERBS AS COMPANION PLANTS

Planted in combination with crops, herbs are also extremely effective at repelling specific insects and pests.

HERB	PLANT NEXT TO OR NEAR:
basil	tomatoes
bay leaves	beans
borage	strawberries, tomatoes
catnip	eggplants (aubergines)
chamomile	cabbages, onions
chives	carrots
cilantro	all vegetables
dill	cabbages
feverfew	roses
garlic	raspberries, roses
hyssop	cabbages
mint	cabbages, tomatoes
nasturtium	cabbages, pumpkins, radishes
oregano	brassicas
rosemary	beans, cabbages, carrots
sage	cabbages, carrots
thyme	cabbages

TOP RIGHT: *green tomatoes on the vine;* CENTER: *pumpkins and squash;* BOTTOM: *fava beans—all are ideal crops for companion planting.*

CHAPTER 4

THE WELL-STOCKED PANTRY

Much of what we buy from a supermarket has traveled on average 12,500 miles (20,000 kilometers). One day we might find ourselves in the situation where oil has become so extortionately expensive that the idea of our food traveling so far to reach our plates is ludicrous (even without oil being prohibitively expensive, the idea is ludicrous). We might find our plates empty unless we rediscover the skills needed to produce food ourselves, locally, organically, safely, and sustainably. Whether we are growing food ourselves or we are shopping for food, it would be an enormous contribution to lessening the effects of global warming if we were, as much as we possibly can, to shop locally, seasonally, and organically.

Local producers and supermarkets

I have to admit that I often find myself in a supermarket. I am not suggesting that supermarkets are an expendable commodity —they have a place in our time-restricted lives. However, more consideration should be taken as to where they are located, the way they treat their suppliers, and the damage they do to the business of smaller, local stores. I do believe that the resurgence of specialist food stores and farmers' markets is proving that we do understand that eating seasonal, locally produced food is an important factor in reducing our carbon footprint.

LEFT, BELOW, AND RIGHT: *Supermarket packaging is responsible for 4.6 million tons of waste generated every year in Britain alone. It is us who buy, and dispose of the packaging, and it is therefore up to us to stop buying such over-packaged produce. Produce bought at farmers' markets is usually wrapped in paper or placed right into your shopping basket or bag.*

For me, buying food from a supermarket is something I am not proud of, since I am fortunate enough to live in an area surrounded by farmers' markets and locally run farm shops, and I grow my own fruit and vegetables. Like many others, I justify my actions by shortage of time and a disorganized head full of deadlines. My failing eyesight renders me completely blind to the tiny writing on packaging. The other day I bought broccoli wrapped in plastic, flown in from Spain—I blush with shame as I write. There is spinach, lettuce, Swiss chard, and asparagus in my garden. I wanted to buy lamb; but, searching the meat cabinet, I could find only imports from New Zealand. I asked an assistant why, in this corner of England, surrounded by farmland particularly suited to rearing sheep, did they not stock English lamb? The reply: "We are having difficulty finding a supply."

Seasonal food

Whether you live in a city, a town, a suburb, or the country, there should always be a supply of indigenous food—we only have to look for it, or to ask for it. The time has come for us to realize the great impact of having nonseasonal produce in our shops, and of imported food replacing what we can grow easily on our own doorstep.

To wait for the local strawberry season is not a hardship. We should and must ask ourselves whether a bowl of strawberries flown in from hundreds of miles away is a necessary extravagance. Apart from the air miles, the electricity used in keeping the fruits fresh and the task of distribution from central storage areas, more often than not the fruit is tasteless because it has been picked too early. In Britain every year, supermarkets import strawberries from Spain and other southern regions before English strawberries are available. This summer my local supermarket offered strawberries flown in from the United States—several thousand miles away! I do not question the quality of this fruit; I do object to the fact that supermarket fruit buyers don't seem to understand the huge impact their buying strategies are having on our world—all in the name of commerce.

The traditional pantry

To make use of seasonal foods without daily trips to the supermarket, a good pantry is essential. In Britain, where refrigerators are typically quite small (what Americans call a "compact refrigerator"), the traditional pantry—or larder, as we British call it—still performs a useful function in many homes. The pantry is a cool room, usually adjacent to the kitchen, where foods such as fresh produce that needn't be kept refrigerator-cold, can be stored. It's also useful for putting cooked dishes that should be allowed to cool down before being refrigerated, in order to avoid using so much electricity.

On the other side of the Pond, big fridges have largely done away with the need for a larder, although a pantry (from the French *paneterie*, for storing bread) survives in modified form, as a place to store dry and canned foods. This can be just an area of the kitchen or the utility room, fitted with lots of shelves and concealed with one or more doors. But if you're lucky enough to have a separate room to use as a pantry, I recommend keeping it cool, so that you can use it to pre-chill cooked dishes and as temporary cool storage over holidays, when the fridge is full to bursting.

Pantry ingredients

Keep your pantry stocked with the following items:

Necessities for preserving:
- vinegar
- sugar
- coarse salt
- spices
- dried herbs
- collection of recycled jam jars

RIGHT: *The simple things in life—good bread and good butter.*

FAR RIGHT: *Garlic—a simple, easy-to-grow bulb, with many health-giving properties (see page 153).*

For rainy days and hungry guests:

- dried beans—chickpeas, flageolets, navy (haricot), kidney
- dried fruit—apricots, currants, raisins, etc.
- jars and jars of homemade jams, jellies, chutneys, and other relishes
- organic cooking chocolate industrial quantities)
- organic flour
- organic oats—for cooking, baking, and bathing (see page 163)
- organic pasta—a good selection of sizes and shapes
- organic tomatoes—canned or bottled
- organic dried yeast

Produce to grow in huge quantities because it stores well:

- apples
- beets (beetroot)
- garlic
- nuts
- onions and shallots
- potatoes
- small fruits
- tomatoes—to use fresh, in chutneys or in sauces

Food items to buy when you don't know what to buy:

- lemons—for a million reasons
- organic butter
- organic eggs
- organic milk and cream

Harvesting and storing

The most important rule in the storing of produce, whether bought or grown yourself, is to store only perfect fruits and vegetables. When harvesting, separate any damaged fruit or vegetables and use immediately; dispose of anything that looks infected on a bonfire. Perfect specimens are less likely to deteriorate in storage and more likely to keep for months.

Pick vegetables at their optimum size—the younger, the better —over a period of time. The aim is to avoid finding yourself picking old, stringy vegetables or gigantic peas, because the effort involved in preserving them will be somewhat wasted. Remember that the more young, succulent vegetables you pick, the more the plant will respond by producing more.

Storing vegetables
When the garden is producing more than you and your family can eat, try these storage methods for putting food by for winter months.

Beans and peas
Dry and store beans and peas, or blanch them in lightly salted water and freeze. To blanch, bring a pan of water to the boil, add the vegetables, and bring back to the boil for one minute. Drain and plunge them immediately into ice-cold water, and drain again—this will preserve their beautiful bright green color. Shake them dry, then seal them in bags and put into the freezer immediately.

Garlic
As with onions, it is important to store dry, perfect specimens. If they are less than perfect, use right away. Keeping the long stalks intact is the perfect method of storage. Once you have braided the stalks together into a long rope, hang in a cool, dark place.

Onions
Harvest onions when most of the tops have fallen over and begun to wilt and dry. Pull or dig the bulbs out carefully with the tops attached. After harvesting, dry or cure the onions in a warm, dry, well-ventilated location,

A WELL-STOCKED FREEZER
One of the few modern-day inventions that can make up for their carbon footprint in usefulness is the freezer. Well stocked and efficiently run, it can save many a trip to the supermarket. It is also invaluable for storing seasonal fruit and vegetables from the garden or from the market, to keep you fed throughout the winter months.

dried apple rings

This is a simple yet effective way to store apples for cooking. The dried apple rings can be kept for use throughout the winter, and are ideal for pies and apple sauces.

you will need
Apples (with no bruises)
Apple corer and sharp knife
Sturdy string
Freezer bag

1 Using only perfect fruit with no bruising, peel and core the apples. Then slice them to make rings ¼–½ in. (5mm–1cm) thick.

2 Thread the apple rings onto a length of sturdy string and hang them in a warm, dry place.

3 When the apple rings are perfectly dry, seal them in a plastic bag, making sure all the air is expelled, and store them in a cool, dark place.

4 When you come to use them, put them in a saucepan with a small amount of water, bring to the boil and simmer until they are reconstituted. Then include them in your recipe as you would fresh apples.

such as a shed or garage. If the weather is sunny, leave onions outside to dry but cover them at night so they don't get damp in the morning dew.

Cure the onions for two to four weeks until the tops and necks are thoroughly dry and the outer bulb scales begin to rustle. After the onions are properly cured, cut off the tops about 1 inch (2.5cm) above the bulbs. As you cut off the tops, discard any onions that show signs of decay. Use the thick-necked bulbs immediately, as they don't store well.

Place the cured onions in a mesh bag, wicker basket, wire basket, or crate (or braid them together so that they can be hung) and store them in a cool, dry location such as a garage, potting shed, or cool basement. In particularly cold climes, the temperature in an unheated garage or shed may fall well below freezing. If such extreme weather is expected, bring the onions inside until the temperature rises.

The storage life of onions is determined by the variety and storage conditions. Good keepers, such as "Sweet Sandwich," that are properly stored should keep for several months. Onions will sprout if the storage temperatures are too warm, and they may deteriorate in damp locations.

Although onions are easy to grow and it is satisfying to store enough to cover your needs for several months, they are also cheap and easy to buy, so I wouldn't get too stressed about their storage.

Root crops

The traditional method of storing root crops, such as potatoes, parsnips, and beets, is known in Britain as clamping. It involves making a pyramid from straw and earth beaten flat with the back of a shovel. However, in this day and age we can probably manage with other, less arduous methods. Sturdy paper grocery bags are adequate for storing root vegetables and are easily obtainable. Vegetables stored in this manner must be dry and in perfect condition at the outset. Store in cool, dry, and dark conditions—a cold garage or a north-facing pantry is a perfect location.

Corn

Boil corn cobs in water for 15 minutes, then dry in a slow oven overnight. Cut the kernels off the cobs, seal them in jars, and store in a cool, dark place. To use them, just boil in salted water until tender.

LEFT: *If you leave the long stalks on drying onions and garlic, they can be braided together to make a long string (start braiding from the bulb end) and hung in a cool place to store.*

RIGHT: *Store only perfect specimens of potato, make sure they are dry and kept in a dark, cool place. Never eat potatoes with green areas—this is caused by storing potatoes in the light.*

Storing fruit

Although the best option is always to eat fruit fresh from the garden, part of the pleasure of growing your own crops, or buying seasonally during the short window of excess, is that you can store a good supply for the dreary winter months.

At certain times of year the garden is laden with goodies. In the summer, strawberries, blueberries, red currants, loganberries, and raspberries are almost overwhelmingly plentiful. Later in the year, apples, crab apples, pears, and quinces become abundant.

Apples

You can store apples for as long as four months, but each fruit must be in good condition with no sign of bruising or insect damage. Wrap each one separately in newspaper (the black-and-white pages, not the color sections) to prevent any mold or bacteria from spreading. Store in special wooden apple racks or baskets in a cool, dry, dark place. Early ripening varieties are best used right away. You can also dry apples cut into rings—see page 123 for details.

LEFT: *Wrap each apple individually in newspaper to prevent the spread of disease.*

RIGHT: *Ripe apples, ready for picking and storing for winter use.*

STORING NUTS

Due to their high fat content, nuts are susceptible to going rancid, so the best way to store shelled nuts is in sealed jars or bags, kept in the freezer. This does them no harm, and they will keep for up to eight months. Nuts easily absorb odors from their surroundings—another reason for keeping them in isolation in cold storage. Always taste stored nuts before using them, because if they have turned rancid, they will spoil the entire dish.

Small fruits

Small fruits can be stewed; made into pies, jellies, jams, and cordials; or frozen. Small fruits, such as red currants, blackberries, and raspberries, respond well to freezing. Firstly inspect each fruit, removing leaves and any creatures, and wipe clean. Segregate any bad or damaged fruits and either use immediately or put on the compost heap. Spread out fruits on a flat baking pan or tray that will fit into the freezer easily. Freeze in batches, making sure each fruit lies separately. It will not take very long to freeze these little individual fruits, and once they are solid, they can be decanted into bags and stored.

If you have gathered blackberries from roadside bushes, before using soak them for five minutes in a solution of cold water to which you have added two tablespoons of distilled white vinegar. This will remove the effects of road pollution.

LEFT: *Frozen raspberries are lovely in summer drinks. Used instead of ice cubes, they will flavor the drink as they slowly thaw.*

TOP RIGHT: *Straw placed under strawberry crops will deter slugs and keep the fruits clean during rainfall, preventing mud and dirt from contaminating them.*

CENTER RIGHT: *Raspberry bushes can provide fruit throughout the summer and well into fall across several different fruiting varieties.*

BOTTOM RIGHT: *Blackberries growing wild in a hedge.*

petal sugar

Flavored sugars have all sorts of uses in cooking, and are an unusual—and delightful—addition to the pantry. For instance, rose petal sugar can be added to soufflés, and the petals of sweet violet make a delicately scented sugar to sprinkle on cakes and pastries. Alternatively, herbs, such as rosemary, can be used as flavoring, and the versatile lavender has a distinctive taste. Make sure all herbs or flowers are clean, dry, and untainted by chemical sprays before making the sugar.

you will need
Rose petals
Fine granulated sugar
2 airtight jars
Sieve

1 In a clean, dry, airtight jar, alternate a layer of fine granulated sugar with a layer of rose petals.

2 When the jar is full, close it and leave in a cool, dark place for one to two weeks.

3 After that time, sieve the sugar to remove all traces of the petals or herbs.

4 Pour into another airtight jar, seal and keep in the pantry until you're ready to use it.

Preserves, jams, jellies, and drinks

When you find yourself with a glut of fruit and want to preserve some of your crop, or when produce is in season and therefore cheaper, make some jam or jelly. Jam making is a tradition well worth keeping alive. The pleasure you get from ranks of jam jars filled with jams, jellies, and relishes, shiny and dark, lined up in the pantry is hard to measure.

Homemade preserves also make a lovely gift. In fact, any homemade gift is so much more meaningful than something bought in a store. Once you have made jams and look lovingly at the "fruits" of your labor, it is indeed quite hard to give them away. A gift of homemade jam is so precious that you might become quite mean-spirited and need to think hard about whether the recipient is deserving enough! A clever way around this mean-spiritedness is to make sure you keep a stock of small preserve jars—particularly sweet are the miniature versions of the "Le Parfait" spring-lidded jars. It is easier to part with a little jar than a whopping great one, especially if you have even the slightest doubt as to whether it will be truly appreciated.

To make up for that rather cruel and selfish last paragraph, may I suggest that a more interesting—not to mention generous— gift would be to present a selection of jams packed in a box.

The recipes for preserves in this chapter come from a variety of tried and tested sources. Most of them have been passed on to me by my mother, who, in turn, inherited them from her mother. The secret of making preserves is to follow the recipes in minute detail, measure the fruit and sugar carefully and follow the timings.

CANNING JARS
Although it is quite possible to use ordinary jars for preserving food, the use of special canning jars, called mason jars after their inventor, is recommended. These have a rubber seal, which ensures that the contents are airtight. Among the most popular brands around are Ball, in the United States, and Le Parfait, in Europe.

RIGHT: *The jewel-like hues of home-made jams and jellies—stored in the pantry, they will see you through the winter months.*

Jam-making equipment

Jam pan Although you can prepare fruit in an ordinary large saucepan, a special jam pan will make the job easier. These pans are wider at the top than at the bottom, which makes the evaporation process much quicker than in a normal saucepan, This is especially useful for reducing vinegar when making chutney.

Jars You will need mason jars in suitable sizes. The jars and lids (but not the screw-on bands) must be sterilized before use—either in a dishwasher or in a large saucepan of water brought to the simmer (fill the jars with water to prevent them from floating). Or place them in water in a roasting pan in a moderate oven for 10 minutes. Leave the jars and lids in the hot water until you are ready to fill them.

Water canner This can be any large saucepan or pot that will accommodate several mason jars. It should have a lid and a rack (this can be a cake rack) on which the jars can stand.

Jelly strainers Jellies need to be strained. You can buy a jelly strainer from specialist cooking stores, but I think they look rather disgusting after use because it is difficult to wash them well. Instead, invest in a large sieve and line it with muslin or cheesecloth—this is a much simpler and less unruly method.

Other equipment A wide-mouthed funnel is required for pouring preserves into the jars. You will also need tongs, for handling the jars and hot lids. A rubber spatula is useful for removing air bubbles. Have ready several dish towels, on which to place filled jars. You'll also need adhesive labels for identifying the contents.

RIGHT: *Jars for canning are useful for storing a variety of things, from jams to cleaning products.*

Processing

Remove a sterilized jar from the hot water and fill it with preserves, leaving ¼–½ in. (5–12mm) space at the top. Remove any air bubbles with the spatula. Place a lid on top, and screw on the band (not too tightly). Repeat with other jars, and place them in the canner. Fill the canner with water to cover the jars by at least 1 in. (2.5cm). Cover the canner with the lid, bring the water to a full boil, and leave for 15 minutes (or more, according to the recipe).

Remove the jars from the water, using tongs to avoid burning your fingers, and place them on a folded towel. Leave them for at least 12 hours, then test the seal by removing the band and attempting to lift the lid. If you cannot lift it with your fingers, the seal is secure. Replace the bands, label the jars, and store them in a cool, dark, dry place.

Useful hints for jam making

Preparing and selecting fruit Make sure the fruit you choose is dry. If the fruit is wet, the pectin naturally present in fruit will be diluted and the jam will not set satisfactorily. Underripe fruit contains more pectin and fruit acid (which helps the setting process) than overripe fruit.

Preserving sugar You can buy special preserving sugar with added pectin to help jam set well.

Testing the setting point When you think the jam is at setting point, spoon a little onto a cold saucer, and leave for a few minutes. If it forms a crinkled skin when pushed with your finger, it has reached setting point.

BELOW: *Jars partly filled with water and placed in a roasting pan for sterilizing in the oven.*

Strawberry jam

This recipe is good for using up a glut of fruit during the strawberry season. The jam will keep for several months.

4 lb. (1.8kg) slightly underripe dry strawberries, hulled
5½ cups (1.3kg) sugar
Juice of 2 large lemons
2 teaspoons (10g) butter

Layer the hulled strawberries in a jam pan with the sugar, and leave overnight. By the morning the sugar will have almost dissolved. Shake the pan to distribute the fruit and juices. Place on low heat, and without stirring too much (shake it a bit as professional cooks do) wait until the sugar has completely dissolved. At this point add the lemon juice and turn up the heat. When the jam has boiled for about 8 minutes, remove from the heat.

Meanwhile, chill a few saucers in the refrigerator for testing the set. Sterilize 6 jars (see page 134).

To test for setting point, spoon a small amount of the jam onto a cold saucer; when cool, test to see whether a light skin has formed by pushing it with your finger. If it has, the jam is ready for canning; if not, boil for a few minutes more, until the cold saucer test works.

Stir in the butter to disperse the scum that will probably have formed. Ladle the jam into the sterilized jars (see page 134), and process as normal (see page 135).

RIGHT: *A good crop of home-grown strawberries, collected in a fine jam pan.*

Blueberry jelly

This is perfect on a croissant—or, of course, on a blueberry muffin.

2 qts. (1kg.) fresh blueberries, rinsed and drained
1 cup (235ml) cold water
1 tablespoon lemon juice
7½ cups (1.7kg) sugar
¾ cup (180ml) liquid pectin

Combine blueberries and water in a saucepan, bring to the boil, and cook until tender. Strain through cheesecloth. You should have about 4 cups (950ml) of juice. Place the juice in a large saucepan or jam pan, and bring to the boil. Boil hard for 5 minutes. Skim the juice if necessary. Add the sugar and lemon juice, and stir to dissolve. Over high heat, bring to a rolling boil, stirring constantly. Add pectin all at once, and boil hard for 1 minute. Remove from heat, skim off foam, and pour into 12 6-oz. (180ml) sterilized jars. Cover with lids and process (see page 135).

Cranberry sauce

A Christmas favorite, cranberry sauce makes a delicious year-round accompaniment to many kinds of meat and some cheeses.

4½ cups (450g) cranberries
2 cups (460g) granulated sugar
2 cups (450ml) water
Grated zest of 1 orange (optional)

Place the sugar and water in a large saucepan and stir to dissolve. Bring to a boil and boil gently for 5 minutes. Add the cranberries and cook until they have finished popping. Add the orange zest, if desired. Pour into 6-oz. (180ml) sterilized jars, and process as normal (see page 135).

RIGHT: *A medlar fruit on the tree.*

Medlar jam

Medlars are inedible until they start to decay. However, they will rarely reach this stage by themselves on the tree and need to be harvested. They should be left outside in a box until they turn a reddish dark brown and have become soft, juicy, and just on the point of rotting. In the seventeenth century this rotting process was known as "bletting" the medlars. Serve this jam with cold meats.

1 lb. (450g) medlars, "bletted"
3¼ cups (760ml) cold water
Sugar
Juice of 1 lemon

Weigh the medlars (the above measurements are a guide). Simmer the "bletted" medlars in the water until soft. Strain through a muslin-lined sieve or jelly bag. Measure the resulting juice and pour into a jam pan. Add 2 scant cups (450g) sugar to every 2½ cups (600ml) of juice extracted from the fruit. Add the lemon juice and bring to the boil until setting point is reached (see page 135). Process as normal (see page 135).

Red currant jelly

Put the red currants into a jam pan and gently heat until the berries have given up their juices. Empty into a sieve lined with cheesecloth or a jelly bag, and allow the juice to drip through. If you like your jellies to have a jewel-like transparency, don't be tempted to squash the fruit through, as this will make your jelly cloudy. Personally I don't have the patience to wait and always end up squishing and pushing just to speed things up a little.

Measure the juice into a jam pan, and add 2 cups (450g) preserving sugar to every 2½ cups (600ml) of juice extracted from the fruit. Stir over low heat until the sugar has dissolved completely. Bring to the boil and boil rapidly until setting point has been reached (see page 135). Pour into sterilized jars (see page 134).

Note: Once jellies have been made, before bottling, add a handful of chopped herbs or whole sprigs of rosemary to the boiling juice just before decanting and sealing.

Crab apple jelly

Inspect the fruit and cut in half; there is no need to peel or core these fruits. Follow the recipe for red currant jelly (above) and for every 2½ cups (600ml) of crab apple juice obtained, add 2 cups (450g) preserving sugar.

Grape jelly

This recipe can use up the grapes that are really too small to eat. Pick the grapes and remove from the stems. Place in a saucepan or jam pan and place on a low heat. Stew until the fruits give up their juice, if necessary adding a small amount of water. Stir and mash with a wooden spoon to help the process along. Put the grape mush into a muslin-lined sieve over a large bowl, and allow the juice to strain. Measure the juice and pour into the pan—for every 2½ cups (600ml) of liquid, add 2 cups (450g) sugar. Bring to the boil until setting point has been reached (see page 135). Pour into sterilized jars and process (see page 135).

ABOVE LEFT: *Grapes—too small for eating—are ideal for turning into grape jelly.*

RIGHT: *Gigantic fruits from the quince tree, waiting to be made into quince jelly.*

Blackberry jelly

Before starting, wash the blackberries (this is especially important if you pick blackberries from roadside, as the fruit may have a coating of grime), then soak for a few minutes in a solution of white vinegar and cold water. Rinse well.

4½ cups (450g) ripe blackberries
¾ cup (180ml) water
2 cups (450g) granulated sugar
Juice of 1 lemon

Put the blackberries in a jam pan with the water, stew gently with lid on for about 25 minutes. Stir and mash, then add the sugar and lemon juice. Continue cooking on a low heat until the sugar has completely dissolved. Working quickly, put the mush into a sieve lined with cheesecloth and swiftly squeeze the jelly through. This jam sets very quickly—if it seems to be setting before it has passed through the sieve, just reheat to melt it and continue putting it through the sieve. Pour into sterilized jars and process (see page 135).

Quince jelly

Quince, known as *marmelo* in Portuguese, was once the main ingredient in marmalade. Quinces had not been replaced by oranges until the nineteenth century.

2 lb. (900g) quinces, peeled, cored, and sliced
(prepared weight)
3¾ cups (900ml) water
Juice of 1 lemon
Sugar

Place the quinces in a jam pan, add the water and simmer gently until tender and mushy. Add the sugar and stir until dissolved; boil until setting point has been reached (see page 135). Process as usual (see page 135).

Raspberry and herb cordial

To make the ice cubes, simply place a small herb sprig in each compartment of an ice-cubetray, cover with water, and freeze.

9 cups (1kg) raspberries
Juice of 1 lemon, or more to taste
2 cups (450g) sugar, or to taste
Ice cubes made with a sprig of herb (rosemary,
hyssop, mint)

Carefully pick over the raspberries and place in a jam pan. Slowly bring to the boil, stirring all the time until the fruit has given up its juice. Pour into a sieve lined with cheesecloth and press the juice through. Return the juice to the pan and add the lemon juice and sugar; stir over a low heat until the sugar has dissolved. Decant into dry, sterilized bottles (see page 134), and store in the refrigerator until required. Serve cold with sparkling water and herb ice cubes.

LEFT: *Homemade cordials, using the fruits of your labor.*

RIGHT: *Sloe gin makes a lovely gift.*

BELOW: *Freeze sprigs of herbs with water in ice-cube trays to flavor and chill drinks on hot summer days.*

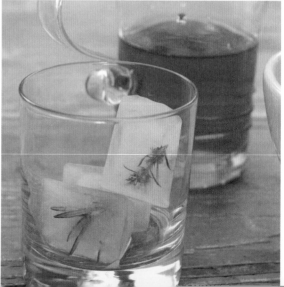

Blackberry cordial

Put the cleaned and de-stalked fruits in a bowl, and cover with two parts water and one part white wine vinegar. Leave in a cool place for two or three days. Strain the blackberries and place in a saucepan along with 2 cups (450g) of sugar to every 1 lb. (450g) of fruit. Boil until the fruit is melted and the sugar dissolved. Strain through cheesecloth and bottle; the blackberry cordial will keep for several weeks in the refrigerator.

Sloe gin

Never having made sloe gin, I was struck by the beauty of a heavy crop of sloes (blackthorn; *Prunus spinosa*) growing in my garden and I was moved to turn the dark, plum-colored berries into Christmas gifts. The recipe is simple and the results delicious, even after only a day. If sloes are unavailable, blackberries or raspberries make a good substitute.

3¼ lb. (1.5kg) sloes
8 cups (2 liters) gin
¾ cup (175g) fine granulated sugar, or to taste—I added a lot more, but I have a very sweet tooth

If you have the patience and the recipients have the delicate palate to notice, prick each sloe with a needle to release the flavor.

Sterilize large glass jars (see page 134). I like to use either Le Parfait canning jars (see page 132) or a collection of beautiful antique bottles with openings large enough to put the sloes into. Divide the sloes between the bottles, pour in the sugar, and fill with gin. Remember to leave enough space for the contents to be shaken periodically. Seal the bottles and leave to brew for three months.

You are supposed to decant the contents, but personally I think that the sloes left inside the bottle look rather beautiful.

Apple relish (chutney)

This is a good recipe to make in the fall, as it uses up any unripe green tomatoes and windfall cooking apples.

4 lb. (1.8kg) green tomatoes
1 teaspoon salt
1 lb. (450g) cooking apples
1¼ lb. (550g) shallots
1 lb. (450g) red tomatoes
2 red bell peppers
2½ cups (450g) brown sugar
1⅓ cups (300ml) cider vinegar

Slice the green tomatoes thinly and sprinkle with salt. Leave for an hour or two. Peel, core, and chop the apples and the shallots. Slice and remove the hard core of the red tomatoes. Put the peppers under the broiler or in the oven to make removing the skin easier. Discard the core and seeds, then peel and chop. Rinse the green tomato slices and shake dry in a sieve. Put all ingredients except the peppers and the red tomatoes into a jam pan and bring to the boil. Simmer for 20 minutes or until the liquid has evaporated. Add the peppers and red tomatoes. Simmer until thick. Pour into sterilized jars and process (see page 135).

Oven-dried tomatoes

Halve the tomatoes and scoop out the seeds. Make a paste with finely chopped garlic, basil leaves, extra-virgin olive oil, freshly ground black pepper, and coarse salt and spread the mixture onto the tomato shells. Place in a shallow baking dish and leave in a low oven for 2–3 hours.

Herb oils and vinegars

The recipe works for both herb vinegars and oils. Use white wine vinegar, as it is light and will absorb the flavor of the herb's own oil well. Any fresh culinary herb can be used. Feed sprigs of fresh herbs through the neck of the bottle of vinegar or oil. Seal and store in a cool, dark place for up to two weeks, then strain, label, and re-bottle in clean bottles.

RIGHT: *Infuse oils and vinegars with herbs. For special gifts, tie a bundle of the dried herb to the bottle. Remove the herbs after a week of infusing, and decant into sterilized bottles.*

BELOW: *Green tomatoes and red peppers add extra flavors to apple relish.*

CHAPTER 5

THE USEFULNESS OF HERBS

Since the life-changing discovery of antibiotics, we have grown to expect quick solutions to our problems. We are demanding antibiotics from our doctors for instant cures for minor ailments that, given time and a strong constitution and the help of something as simple as, for example, garlic, would not only have cured the ailment but also created a more resistant body with its own homegrown antibodies to deal with the next bout of infection. It is estimated that of the 83 million prescriptions issued annually in the United States, outside hospitals, for antibiotics alone, some 50 million are unnecessary. Comparable figures apply in Britain.

Medicinal herbs

Used to treat various ailments since the beginning of time, herbs and flowers are the basis for many modern-day pharmaceutical drugs. Like our ancestors, we discover their benefits by trial and error in scientific research. Two medicinal plants that spring to mind are the yew tree, the toxic berries of which are a vital part of tamoxifen, an estrogen inhibitor used in the treatment or prevention of cancer, and the evening primrose flower, which has many applications in hormonal medicine.

Ancient remedies

For hundreds of years, apothecaries, housewives, and herbalists worked in the "still room," concocting tonics, poultices, and lotions from leaves, flowers, and roots. These were the only medicinal resources available to them for treating and curing illnesses.

During early medieval times the word "herb" denoted all useful plants, which included vegetables as well as herbs as we know them today. It was not until the eighteenth century that herbs were given their own category, distinguishing their medicinal and life-enhancing properties from food plants. Alongside vegetable gardens, infirmary gardens were cultivated to grow specific herbs for the apothecary.

The history of an herb can often be deduced from its traditional name. For instance, the names "woundwort," "blind man's hand," "fairy thimbles", and "friar's-cowl" all tell the tale of their ancient uses. At one time it was thought that the appearance of a plant indicated the part of the body it would heal. Its growing conditions, scent, or special habits provided more clues.

Because adam-and-eve, also known as lungwort (*Pulmonaria officinalis*) bears a resemblance to a diseased lung, it was thought to benefit lung conditions. It is, in fact, an effective expectorant. Allheal (*Prunella vulgaris*) earned its place among healing remedies because the upper "lip" of the flower resembled a hook, which was the main agricultural tool at the time of its discovery in the sixteenth century. Wounds caused by careless use of billhooks and sickles were treated to good effect with allheal.

BE SAFE—SEEK EXPERT GUIDANCE

Herbal medicines can be as powerful as their chemical counterparts prescribed by doctors, so it is absolutely vital that before treating any ailment you SEEK THE ADVICE OF A QUALIFIED HERBAL PRACTITIONER. Synergism —which is the effect caused by combining more than one herbal remedy—can enhance the effect or can make it extremely dangerous. This is another reason why you should always get advice.

Other than as flavoring in cooking, herbs should never be taken during pregnancy or by children under 5 years old.

BELOW: *A wide selection of herbs can be grown in a small container, such as this wooden wine box.*

Sensible use of herbal remedies

As I write, the debate has opened again about the efficacy (or not) of herbal remedies and the qualifications of herbal practitioners. The law on selling herbal remedies that claim to cure ailments is a little cloudy; and as far as I know, the rigorous testing required to license a chemical drug is not applied to herbal alternatives. Be cautious when self-administering herbal preparations, and always confirm your suspicions about ailments with your doctor. Self-diagnosis is fine for minor complaints, but these can be the start of something more serious. Be aware of your body, and any changes you experience, and confirm with your doctor that the herbal preparations you want to take are suitable.

Protecting wild herbs

Interest in herbal medicine is increasing. The more knowledgeable and informed we become about the side effects of conventional medicine, the more we seek alternative remedies—homeopathic, floral, and herbal. This renewed interest has a downside, though. It was always believed that herbs gathered from the wild were more efficacious than cultivated plants, and 90 percent of all herbs used in medicine today are still gathered from the wild. According to the Vegan Society, the herb goldenseal (*Hydrastis canadensis*), used for immune deficiency problems, is now listed by CITES (Convention of Trade in Endangered Species) as the fifth most endangered plant species on the planet. When buying herbal tinctures and preparations, check that all ingredients come from sustainable sources, and that a registered, ecologically sound company manufactures the product.

Growing herbs

The best option is to grow your own herbs and, with the advice and help of your practitioner, make your own remedies. If you find that a specific herb eases symptoms or guards against your particular weaknesses, make sure you have your own sustainable supply. Herbs make beautiful and useful growing companions for flowers, fruit, and vegetables, and in the section on companion planting (see pages 114–115) you will see that their strong scents can not only act as deterrents to pests but also encourage those creatures most likely to feed on any that do persist.

Popular medicinal herbs

The following list includes herbs that are commonly grown or easily found.
I stress again that, unless you are using herbs to flavor food and drinks, you
should seek advice from a herbal practitioner. Never rely solely on home
treatment for any medical complaint. Where appropriate, I have suggested
cures for animals, but take advice from your veterinarian before use.

Aloe Vera

This grows wild in arid regions of Europe,
America and Africa. It will not tolerate frost, but
can be cultivated as an indoor plant in northerly
regions. Personally, I find it rather ugly, but its
healing powers are very effective in the treatment
of sunburn and other minor burns. The gel
extruded when the leaves are cut can be applied
to all sorts of wounds. It forms a protective layer,
encouraging skin regeneration. When ingested,
aloe vera is thought to be an effective intestinal
cleanser. In this case, it is best to buy ready-made
preparations from a reputable source. Aloe vera
is also used in hand creams and shampoo.

Aaron's Rod *(Verbascum thapsus)*

Also known as great mullein, this grows widely
in Europe and North America. It is used to treat
urinary tract and kidney infections, and also to
ease catarrh. Gather the flowering tops of the
plant in summer and dry them. They can be
made into a cold compress that can be used as
an antiinflammatory dressing for wounds and
stings, or into a calming tea.

Allheal *(Prunella vulgaris)*

This plant, also known as self-heal, woundwort
or sticklewort, grows wild throughout temperate
regions of the world and is easy to establish.
Allheal is useful for treating sore throats and
inflammations of the mouth, but its history is
rich and varied. It has been used to treat ailments
from quinsy to diphtheria, and wounds caused
by careless handling of farming tools.

Basil *(Ocimum basilicum)*

The name of this popular herb is derived from
the Greek *Basilikon photon,* which translates as
"kingly herb." However, basil has a mixed, rather
than royal, history—adorning altars in some
Greek Orthodox churches, it has also been
denounced as a plant of the devil. Cultivated for
over 2,000 years, it originated in India, and was
introduced to Mediterranean countries via the
spice routes. Its medicinal uses are limited, but
its oil is said to combat mental fatigue, and
vinegar flavored by its leaves can be added to
bathwater as an antiseptic. Its main use, however,
is in salads and cooking. The leaves aid digestion
as well as adding exotic flavor. The juice of basil
leaves rubbed on skin acts as an insect repellent.

BELOW: *The bright green leaves of basil.*

Celery *(Apium graveolens)*

Although more commonly known as a salad vegetable, celery stems have a calming effect on the gut and are helpful in the detoxification of the kidneys. Eaten raw, celery has a beneficial effect on arthritis.

Chamomile *(Matricaria chamomilla)*

A lovely, low-growing plant, chamomile resembles a daisy. Collect and dry the flowers from June to August. Chamomile is commonly used for its sedative properties, but it also relieves morning sickness, hemorrhoids, mastitis, eczema, and hay fever. When planted in close proximity to ailing plants, chamomile is reputed to help in their recovery.

Cinnamon *(Cinnamomum zeylanicum)*

A spice rather than an herb, cinnamon comes from the bark of the *Cinnamomum verum* tree, native to Sri Lanka and southern India. Its strong flavor is due to the essential oil that makes up 1 percent of its composition. Principally employed in cooking, cinnamon is also used as an insect repellent, to ease the symptoms of colds, and to aid digestive problems; but use it sparingly.

Cloves *(Syzgium aromaticum)*

Cloves, also, are a spice rather than an herb. They have extraordinary healing and pain-relieving powers, and medicinally no other substance has been found to equal their efficacy in relieving toothache. They are also used as a local antiseptic. Lesser known is the effect of cloves on relieving nausea—two drops of the essential oil in water are said to stop vomiting. Cloves stuck into an orange are traditionally used to repel moths.

Comfrey *(Symphytum officinale)*

Also known as Saracen's comfrey. Mainly used in poultices to heal wounds and reduce bruising, comfrey is also used in the treatment of athlete's foot and mastitis. Its leaves contain allantoin, an

HERB TEAS

Both medicinally and for pure pleasure, fresh or dried herbs make a gentle and refreshing alternative to normal tea. Mix with fresh orange or lemon peel for added flavor, and sweeten with honey, if desired. Use one teaspoon for each cup of boiling water, and leave to steep for five minutes.

The following herbs all make delicious teas: basil, caraway, chamomile, elderflower (use only the flowers), fennel, fenugreek, hibiscus, hyssop, lavender (use both the leaves and the flowers), lemon balm, lemon verbena, mint, raspberry leaf, rose petal, rosemary, sage, thyme.

agent that stimulates healthy tissue formation, which probably explains why it is often used in the manufacture of skin-softening cosmetics.

Coriander *(Coriandrum sativum)*

A native of southern Europe and the Middle East, coriander, also called cilantro, was brought to northern Europe by the Romans, who used it with cumin and vinegar as a preservative. Easily grown from seed in light, well-drained soil, coriander thrives in a sunny position and has many culinary uses. Medicinally, coriander leaves aid digestion, reduce flatulence, and stimulate appetite. The dried seeds can be applied in a poultice to relieve painful joints.

Dandelion *(Taraxacum officinale)*

This has many uses, and all of the plant is safe to use. The young leaves, collected before the flowers appear, are good in salads, contain more iron and calcium than spinach, and are rich in vitamins A and C. The leaves are a powerful diuretic, and can be boiled with honey to treat coughs. Dandelions are regarded as one of the best remedies for liver and kidney complaints. The dried roots, dug up in

ABOVE: *Not just a garden weed, dandelion has many uses.*

fall, can be used as a coffee substitute, which acts as a diuretic and is said to cleanse the liver; they are also a mild laxative, and a tonic made from them treats constipation and dyspepsia. The milk from cut flower stems is a mosquito repellent and is said to cure warts. Steeped in boiling water and cooled, dandelions can be used to fertilize plants, as they contain a good supply of copper.

Dill *(Anethum graveolens)*

Remains of this plant have been found in the ruins of Roman buildings in Britain, and it is mentioned in Egyptian herbals dating back more than 5,000 years. Dill is said to improve appetite and aid digestion. Chewing the seeds prevents halitosis, and the crushed seed heads, steeped in hot water, make a nail-strengthening bath.

Elder *(Sambucus nigra)*

Elder flowers, used to make elderflower nectar, or cordial, are beneficial in alleviating catarrh and respiratory complaints. A compress made from the flowers steeped in hot water can be used to ease conjunctivitis, as well as chilblains. A gargle made from an elderflower infusion can soothe sore throats. The flowers can also be infused in vinegar and used in the same way.

Unless cooked, elderberries are *not* to be eaten under any circumstances; even the juice must not be swallowed unless it has been boiled. To make a cure for toothache and migraines, boil the elderberries with a small amount of water, then

BELOW: *Growing herbs in window boxes allows town dwellers an accessible supply of fresh herbs.*

ABOVE: *The feathery fronds of fennel.*

push the mush through a sieve lined with cheesecloth. Measure the juice and return it to the pan, adding 1½ cups (360g) of sugar for each 1 pint (475ml) of juice. Boil, stirring, until the mixture reaches a jam consistency. Bottle in sterilized jars and keep refrigerated until needed. Take two teaspoons when required.

Fennel *(Foeniculum vulgare)*

All parts of the fennel plant are used—the leaves, the seed, and the bulb. As a digestive aid, fennel has been used since the ancient Greeks discovered that it stilled a hungry tummy, and I am delighted to have stumbled upon this as a natural slimming aid. Fennel seeds steeped in water make an aid to digestion, heartburn, and constipation, and a teaspoon of cooled fennel tea comforts babies suffering from colic.

WARNING: fennel essence taken in large doses has been known to cause convulsions and disturb the nervous system.

Feverfew *(Tanacetum parthenium)*

As its name suggests, feverfew was probably used to heal fevers. After extensive clinical trials during the 1970s, it was proven to reduce migraines both in intensity and frequency. The leaves have a very bitter taste—sandwiching

LEFT: *The daisy-like flowers of feverfew.*

two or three small leaves between two slices of bread helps to disguise it. Consult a medical practitioner before taking feverfew, as it is not suitable for everyone, and do not take more than the recommended dose, as this can cause unpleasant side effects. Easily grown, feverfew will self-seed once established.

Garden Violet *(Viola odorata)*

Garden violet flowers are used extensively in the making of perfume, and are also crystallized and used for culinary purposes. Various parts of the plant are used medicinally. The rootstock is made into a soothing expectorant, used to treat respiratory disorders such as bronchitis, coughs, and head colds. Made into a poultice, the leaves soothe sore nipples. The crystallized flowers have a reputation for aiding sleep.

Garlic *(Allium sativum)*

Garlic is such a powerful plant that some risks are associated with it. It is important to remember that with all herbs valued for their medicinal properties, something that benefits one person may be harmful to another.

Botulism (*clostridium botulinum*) presents the most serious risk associated with garlic. The bulb's sulfurous nature makes garlic a breeding ground for this dangerous toxin, which can cause major, sometimes fatal, stomach illness. The danger arises if raw garlic is stored in oil at room temperature or for too long in the fridge, so never store raw garlic this way. When making a salad dressing containing garlic, plan to use it soon after making it. As a rough guide, garlic in oil will keep in the refrigerator for up to two weeks. Fresh cloves can be kept at room temperature for up to a month. It is obvious when garlic is past its prime—it will become soft, its pungency will have weakened, and a green shoot may appear.

RIGHT: *A traditional braid of garlic bulbs.*

Garlic can interfere with certain prescription medicines, especially some anticoagulants used in surgery. In addition, research has concluded that garlic supplements "can cause a potentially harmful side effect when combined with a type of medication used to treat HIV/AIDS."

However, garlic is praised for its cardiovascular benefits and its ability to reduce cholesterol and ward off germs. Because of its strength and power (raw garlic is more potent than cooked) use it wisely, gauge its effects, and don't overindulge.

Honeysuckle *(Lonicera periclymenum)*

Common all over Europe, northern Africa, and North America, honeysuckle is often called woodbine in England. Tea made from its perfumed flowers soothes coughs and asthma. Research has also proved that this tea can be helpful in soothing the pain of colitis. The raw flowers can be used sparingly in salads.

Horseradish *(Armoracia rusticana)*

Both roots and leaves of the horseradish plant are used in cooking. The well-known sauce is made by grating the fresh root, and the young leaves picked in spring can be used in salads. Chopped finely, they can be added to dog and cat food to dispel worms. Horseradish has strong antibiotic properties, and is good for restoring poor circulation. It is also sometimes used as a diuretic for urinary infections, and to relieve rheumatism and gout. A poultice made from fresh grated roots and applied to chilblains or stiff joints and muscles will alleviate discomfort, and is also believed to relieve backache. Over-use of horseradish may cause blisters. Do not use if your thyroid function is low or if thyroxin has been prescribed. Use sparingly if pregnant or suffering from kidney problems.

Hyssop *(Hyssopus officinalis)*

Besides being a delicious addition to a green salad and some kinds of punch, hyssop leaves may be used in infusions to alleviate coughs and asthma or complaints of the upper respiratory tract. Externally, it can be used for bruises and burns and was once used as a remedy for rheumatism.

Although hyssop is safe if used professionally and with care, it should not be used on anyone with nervous irritability. Its distilled oil is not suitable in aromatherapy on patients with a highly strung disposition, as it is capable of causing epileptic fits. Hyssop should never be taken in pregnancy, even in salads or beverages.

Jacob's Ladder *(Polemonium caeruleum)*

This beautiful plant can be propagated from seed or by dividing the plant just after the stalks die down in the fall. Medicinally, the powdered roots and rhizomes can be made into a poultice for bruises, inflammation, and wounds, and the herb is good for dealing with skin blemishes when used as a face wash or for counteracting the effects of poison ivy. Taken internally, the plant is poisonous in its entirety, and to be used only when directed by a qualified herbal practitioner.

Lady's Mantle *(Alchemilla mollis)*

This is also known as silvery lady's mantle. A beautiful plant with green, lobed leaves and greenish-yellow flowers in summer, it thrives and self-seeds in most soils (even in dry gravel and stone walls) but does not do well in wet or boggy ground. The very young leaves can be used in salads. They are slightly bitter but mild in taste.

It is traditionally used for menstrual disorders, and as a mouthwash after a tooth extraction. It can be used to treat diarrhea in pets.

Lavender *(Lavandula angustifolia)*

Growing well in many climes, lavender requires a warm, sunny aspect and well-drained soil, but is as happy in pots as it is in the ground. The flowers deter flies and moths, and the oil made from the leaves has a beneficial effect on stings, burns, cuts, and grazes. Lavender oil has strong antibacterial properties and kills the diphtheria and typhoid bacilli, as well as streptococcus and pneumococcus. Adding the oil to a warm bath helps to assuage depression and anxiety and relieves headaches. Pour a few drops of lavender oil into bathwater to ensure a good night's sleep, or to calm an irritable child.

Lemon Balm *(Melissa officinalis)*

Also known as balm mint, lemon balm is widely grown in Europe and North America, often near orchards, to attract bees. Its medicinal properties include relief from headaches and nervous disorders, such as tension and memory loss. A tea made from the fresh leaves of lemon balm aids digestion, colic, and flatulence. Lemon balm oil is used in aromatherapy to treat depression and sleeplessness. It is a good idea to grow lemon balm in a pot because, like common mint, the roots are very invasive.

Licorice *(Liquiritia officinalis)*

Used medicinally for over 3,000 years, licorice was first discovered by the Greeks. These days it is grown in Russia, Spain, India, and throughout the temperate zones of the world. It became an important crop, used to disguise the unpleasant taste of other medicines while providing a soothing juice to alleviate troublesome coughs.

The dried root, which is stripped of its outer, bitter bark, is used as a remedy for colds, sore throats, and bronchial catarrh. As a gentle remedy for constipation, it also lowers the level of stomach acid and relieves heartburn. Licorice juice is beneficial in healing stomach ulcers, coating the stomach wall and easing spasms of the large intestine. It is also thought to reduce levels of cholesterol in the blood.

RIGHT: *Lavender, ever popular due to its flowers and scent.*

Marigold (Calendula officinalis)

This annual herb thrives in most climes and was first used in Indian and Arabic cultures. Known for its antiseptic, antifungal, and antibacterial properties, it is used in the preparation of calendula cream—a homeopathic remedy effective in treating burns, grazes, scalds, and stings. It is also used in the treatment of varicose veins, chilblains, and impetigo. The petals steeped in boiling water and cooled make an eyewash for the treatment of conjunctivitis, and can be used to relieve the symptoms of thrush. The sap from the stem is said to cure warts, corns, and calluses.

Marjoram (Origanum majorana)

This flowering plant has many species to its name. Also known as oregano in Mediterranean countries, this herb grows wild, as well as being cultivated in pots or beds. The Romans and Greeks used its oils as a disinfectant and as a preservative. Medicinally, it is still used as an antiseptic, owing to its high thymol content. Marjoram tea is a comfort to those suffering from bad colds and has a calming effect

BELOW: *Cough syrup prepared from onions and honey.*

on nerves, as well as helping to settle an upset stomach and relieve seasickness. Like chamomile, marjoram is helpful in aiding restful sleep when a few drops of the essential oil are dripped onto a handkerchief laid on a pillow. Fresh marjoram leaves rubbed on gums soothes toothache.

Nasturtium (Tropaeolum majus)

Also known as Indian cress, this self-seeding and prolific plant is grown worldwide. The deep orange and yellow flowers, which are rich in iron and vitamin C, may be used fresh in salads and as a pretty decoration on ice creams and other desserts. To make a tea, steep the peppery-flavored flowers in boiling water. The flower buds can be pickled in vinegar and used as an alternative to capers.

Nettle (Urtica dioica)

Also called stinging nettle, this seemingly spiteful plant grows prolifically in fertile soil. Use the young spring leaves as a vegetable, cooking them before eating—they are very rich in vitamins and minerals. Nettles are beneficial in the treatment of internal hemorrhages and hemorrhoids, and have a laxative effect. Made into a tonic, nettles can also be used to treat eczema and anemia, providing the right minerals. Their vitamin C content ensures that the minerals are fully absorbed.

Nettles can also be used as an insecticide. Fill a bucket full of nettles, cover with rainwater and steep for a week. Use the liquid in a spray bottle to rid your plants of blackfly and aphids.

Onion (Allium cepa)

Onions of any kind are key ingredients in making a natural cough syrup. Slice the onions and lay them flat in a shallow bowl, drizzle with honey and cover; leave to infuse for two to three hours and drain off the resulting liquid. Administer the syrup by teaspoon to relieve coughs and a tight chest.

Onion flower (Allium ursinum)

Also known as flowering onion, this grows profusely in Europe, Asia, and many countries in the northern hemisphere. The fresh young leaves are delicious in salads and can also be made into soups. Onion flower has been shown to reduce blood pressure, and is therefore beneficial in preventing strokes. It is also used to ease diarrhea and dysentery, tuberculosis, whooping cough, typhoid, and hepatitis, not to mention its beneficial effects in expelling worms. Effective in reducing blood sugar levels, flowering onion can help to control diabetes.

Herbal practitioners use this herb to treat boils, colds, coughs, toothache, earache, and insect bites. It is also traditionally used to make a disinfectant.

Parsley (Petroselinum crispum)

Traditionally used to treat bad breath as the result of eating garlic, the parsley plant is also rich in vitamin C, minerals, and the antiseptic chlorophyll. It can help in relieving urinary infections and, in poultices, acts as an antiseptic dressing for wounds, sprains, and insect bites.

Parsley freezes well and can be used straight from the freezer. Instead of chopping the leaves, you can simply crumble them while frozen.

Peppermint (Mentha piperita)

The leaves of this useful plant are aromatic, antiseptic, antispasmodic, antibacterial and anti-parasitic. The torn leaves steeped in boiling water make a refreshing drink, served either hot or cold with ice. Hot mint tea can relieve headaches and increase ability to concentrate. Mint is helpful in relieving gastro-intestinal disorders, and is an appetite stimulant. It is best to grow mint in pots, because its roots are extremely invasive.

Raspberry leaves

Tea made from dried raspberry leaves is a good cure for diarrhea. Gargle with the tea to soothe a sore throat.

ABOVE: *Rosemary, an herb widely used in cooking.*

Rosemary (Rosmarinus officinalis)

Steeped in myth and magical tales, rosemary was often used to purify the air in the sickroom. Rosemary oil is a very powerful agent and must be used with care and never taken internally. Externally, the oil has antibacterial properties and is said to ease headaches, improve the circulation, and deter insects. Infuse the fresh leaves in boiling water to make a mouthwash for sweet-smelling breath. Taken in small amounts, this infusion also reduces flatulence. Its antibacterial properties make it a good addition to bathwater for healthy skin.

A useful companion plant (see pages 114–115), when grown near carrots, rosemary will repel carrot fly, and it is generally beneficial to sage when planted close by.

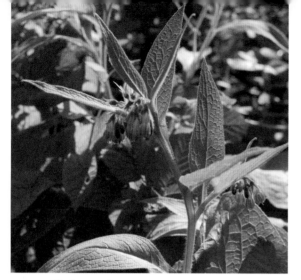

ABOVE: *The leaves of comfrey.*

Sage *(Salvia officinalis)*

Medicinally, this plant is highly regarded. Also known as salvia, from the Latin *salveo*, meaning "I save," it is used to treat colds and, when made into a tisane with a little cider vinegar, is effective as a gargle to treat sore throat, laryngitis, and tonsillitis. The mouthwash may also be used to treat mouth ulcers and infections of the gums.

Saint-John's-Wort *(Hypericum perforatum)*

Also known as herb of Saint John, this herb has yellow flowers, which were once credited with curing cases of mania. It is still used to alleviate depression, but dependence upon drugs made from this herb has been known, and it should be administered only by a qualified practitioner. Stopping treatment must be done under supervision.

Externally, the oil extracted from the flowers may be applied to ease neuralgia, varicose veins, and ulcers. It also relieves sunburn.

To grow Saint-John's-Wort, sow seeds in the spring where you want the plant to flower—it is very hardy and spreads easily by self-seeding, so keep cutting back to prevent it from taking over.

Sweet Woodruff *(Gallium odoratum)*

This herb was once used to scent linen and stuff mattresses. Medicinally, it is made into a tea that is said to relieve stomach pain. It will also act as an effective diuretic.

A hardy perennial, this herb has pretty, star-shaped flowers, which can be used sparingly in salads. It can be grown in pots, but quickly becomes pot bound. Consumption of large quantities can produce symptoms of poisoning, including dizziness and vomiting, so use with care.

Thyme *(Thymus spp.)*

Although thyme grows prolifically in the wild, it can be cultivated in pots and in herb gardens. There are hundreds of species, and many of them prefer poor, free-draining soil. The tiny leaves give off a pungent, heady scent in the heat. Used in cooking, the oils break down fatty foods, particularly in oily fish dishes and stews. Thyme has strong antiseptic properties, and the essential oil, which is toxic and must never be ingested, is also antibacterial and antifungal. A few drops used in bathwater is said to relieve the pain of rheumatism. Avoid completely if pregnant.

Vervain *(Verbena officinalis)*

Said to have been used to stem the flow of Christ's blood at the Crucifixion, vervain is also known as holy herb. Vervain has been used to ease nervous exhaustion and depression for hundreds of years, and is now also used in the treatment of liver problems and urinary tract infections.

Yarrow *(Achillea millefolium)*

Creeping rootstock ensures that yarrow, also known as woundwort, survives whatever situation it may find itself in, and it is common all over the world, usually on waste ground. Medicinally, it is one of the best-known remedies for curing fevers. Used as an infusion, it induces sweats that cool fevers and expel toxins. The Chinese use it in a poultice for healing wounds.

Yarrow also encourages fast decomposition of waste vegetation, making it an essential, albeit not very beautiful, addition to the organic garden.

bouquet garni herbs

Little muslin bags of bouquet garni seem to have all but disappeared from our lives. If used right away, fresh herbs are more potent, but dried ones keep longer. A selection specially prepared to suit different foods, presented in a box, makes a lovely gift. Add your own favorite recipes using each one to make it even more special.

you will need

Selection of herbs
String
Muslin
Ribbon
Decorative box
Tissue paper

1 Gather a selection of herbs, tie them around the stems in small bunches, and hang up to dry.

2 Cut some muslin squares, about 8 x 8 in. (20 x 20cm).

3 Place some dried herbs on each muslin square—use the list below for guidance.
For chicken: chives, thyme, and rosemary
For game: juniper berries, rosemary, and bay leaves
For lamb: rosemary or lemon thyme and parsley
For beef: thyme with lemon thyme or bay
For pork: rosemary or sage with parsley
For tomato dishes: oregano, parsley, and chives
For potatoes: sage with bay or thyme

4 Gather each muslin square at the corners and tie with ribbon or string.

5 Put them in a decorative box, lined with tissue paper.

Homemade medicinal preparations

For minor complaints and for alternatives to such products as insect repellent, it is safe to make your own preparations.

Sage lotion for sunburned skin
Tear a handful of fresh sage leaves into a bowl, cover with boiling water and infuse for 20 minutes. Strain into a bottle, refrigerate, and apply when needed.

Saint-John's-Wort lotion
The mashed yellow flowers of Saint-John's-Wort mixed with olive oil make a soothing lotion for sunburn or varicose veins.

Peppermint oil for muscular pain
To relieve sore muscles, massage the affected area with peppermint oil. If you use a commercial oil, check that it is suitable for external use.

Basil mosquito repellent
Simply crush basil leaves and rub them onto areas of exposed skin to repel mosquitoes.

Disinfect with feverfew
To disinfect slight wounds and to aid sleep, gather dried or fresh feverfew flowers in cheesecloth bath bags (see page 163) and add to bathwater.

Removing nits from hair
Soak your hair in neat white distilled vinegar, wrap it in a towel for an hour, then comb with a nit comb to remove the creatures before washing your hair again. Finish with another coating of vinegar without rinsing off—this leaves hair glossy and shiny. Combing neat vodka through hair also removes nits.

Combat hair loss
Drink a banana smoothie made from mashed bananas, honey, yogurt, and low-fat milk regularly; this mixture is rich in biotin, which is said to prevent hair loss.

MEDICINAL USES FOR WHITE DISTILLED VINEGAR

Bee stings To soothe bee stings hold a cotton pad soaked in vinegar on the affected part.

Blocked sinuses Make a vaporizer by adding a quarter cup of vinegar to steaming water, and inhale the fumes to help clear sinuses.

Burns Keep a container of vinegar in the fridge, and apply to minor burns to relieve pain.

Sunburn To soothe sunburn, apply vinegar with a soft pad of cotton.

Dandruff To rid the scalp of dandruff, use a solution of half a cup of vinegar and two cups of warm water.

Sore throats To soothe a sore throat, gargle with a glass of water to which you have added two tablespoons of vinegar.

Hot toddies If you don't have a lemon to add to a hot toddy for soothing a cold, use vinegar and honey in hot water.

cucumber lotion

Homegrown, organic cucumber makes a deliciously cool lotion, especially for the face—marvelous for hot summer days. It's also very soothing when applied to sunburned skin. Keep a bottle of the lotion in the fridge. Use within two weeks.

you will need

Fresh cucumber
Sieve
Fine cheesecloth
Glass jar or spray bottle
Eau de cologne

1 Coarsely grate a firm, fresh cucumber and place in a sieve lined with fine cheesecloth.

2 Place the sieve over a bowl and push the cucumber through the cheesecloth to release the juice.

3 Pour the resulting liquid into a clean glass jar or spray bottle.

4 Add a few drops of eau de cologne for a scented lotion, and apply as required.

Homemade beauty preparations

You will find that your pantry essentials (see pages 120–121) are not just useful in the kitchen, but in the bathroom as well. Many bath and beauty preparations will benefit from the addition of fresh or dried herbs.

For the bath

Making your own bath preparations is very simple, will save you a great deal of money, and will ensure that you are bathing in the purest of ingredients.

Basic body scrub

Smooth, blemish-free skin is easily achieved with the help of just a few basic ingredients. You can be sure that homemade scrubs are pure, with no added chemicals, and can be custom made to suit all types of skin.

⅝ cup (225g) coarse salt crystals
4 tablespoons olive oil
juice of 1 lemon or lime

Mix all the ingredients together and rub all over the body once a week to exfoliate skin, concentrating on problem areas, such as knees, feet, and elbows; then shower off. The lime or lemon juice in the mixture acts as a bleaching agent, which will whiten your finger- and toenails. The scrub can also be used as a cuticle softener, on both feet and hands.

For extra therapeutic benefits, add some fresh or dried herbs to your body scrub. My suggestions are:
- comfrey, for rejuvenation and softening of the skin
- lavender flowers, to promote restful sleep
- elderflowers steeped in water, to whiten and soften the skin, and to lighten freckles
- mint, for a fresh and invigorating sense of well-being
- rosemary, to invigorate and energize
- vervain, to alleviate nervous exhaustion
- thyme, for its antibacterial properties.

Refreshing morning bath tonic

For an extremely invigorating tonic, add crushed wormwood leaves to cider vinegar and leave to infuse. Store in a glass jar with a nonmetallic lid. Add this to running bathwater in the morning for a fresh start to the day.

Bath teas

Infuse fresh bay leaves in boiling water and add the strained bay tea to a hot bath to relieve aching limbs. For healthy skin, pour a cup of strong rosemary tea into bathwater.

Deep cleanse with fennel

For really deep cleansing, use fennel seeds and leaves with oatmeal in your bath bag (see facing page for instructions).

oatmeal bath bags

Organic oatmeal flakes make a wonderful skin softener when added to bathwater. Make a selection, and if you can bear to, give some away as presents; but be sure to indulge yourself as well.

you will need

Cheesecloth
Organic oatmeal
Herbs, either flowers or sprigs
Ribbon or string

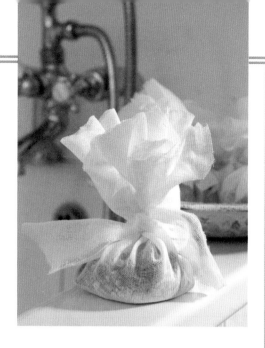

1 Cut some squares of cheesecloth each measuring approximately 8 x 8 in. (20 x 20cm).

2 Place a handful of oat flakes together with some herb flowers, or a sprig or two of your chosen herb, on each square of cheesecloth. Gather up the corners and tie securely with ribbon or string to form a bag.

3 Make the ribbon long enough to tie to the faucet so that the running hot water deluges the bag. Alternatively, just drop the bag in the bath, immersing it in the water, and squeeze it gently until the water turns milky soft.

LEFT AND BELOW: *Coarse salt not only makes an excellent exfoliant, but also softens bathwater. Fill jars with natural coarse salt and add either olive oil or a scented oil. Lavender oil makes very beautiful bath salts and, if used at night, will promote restful sleep. Other herbs, oils and fresh or dried flowers can be added to make unique customized bath salts—try rosemary oil with a sprig of rosemary, or rose oil with dried rosebuds. If using fresh herbs or flowers, use within one or two weeks, before the flower petals or leaves lose their color.*

Hair and scalp

To improve the condition of your scalp and make your hair strong and shiny, experiment with the following herbal treatments.

Brightening fair hair

Steep the leaves of betony in hot water to make a yellow dye that will highlight light-colored hair. Chamomile water in the final rinse is also good for fair hair—pour boiling water over fresh chamomile flowers, leave for an hour, and use when cooled.

Adding shine to dark hair

Rosemary tea as a final rinse leaves dark hair shiny and glossy.

Nettle scalp tonic

Not only do nettles have a good reputation for encouraging hair growth; they also eliminate dandruff. Boil a large rubber-gloved handful of nettles in water and simmer for 10 minutes, cool, and strain the liquid. Store it in the fridge and use when required.

Horsetail hair tonic

A common and invasive weed, horsetail may be growing, uninvited, in your garden. Steep a bunch of horsetail in simmering water for 20 minutes. This decoction can be used as a tonic to strengthen your hair. After shampooing, rinse and pour a pitcherful of cooled horsetail water over your hair, wrap your head in a warm towel for 20 minutes, then rinse. The lotion can also be used as a nail strengthener.

Parsley seed hair tonic

Crush parsley seeds and steep them in water to make a hair rinse that will leave hair shiny and glossy. It is also said to eliminate head lice. Pour the rinse over your head and wrap in a towel for an hour. Do not rinse off, and allow hair to dry naturally.

Malt vinegar hair tonic

To add a glowing shine to your hair, add half a cup of malt vinegar to the final rinse.

Dry shampoo

If you have no time to shampoo your hair before going out, dust it with talcum powder or corn starch and brush it out. Try this out first when you are not in a hurry to make sure that it works in the way you want.

BELOW: *Often found growing in the wild, nettles make a wonderful tonic for the scalp.*

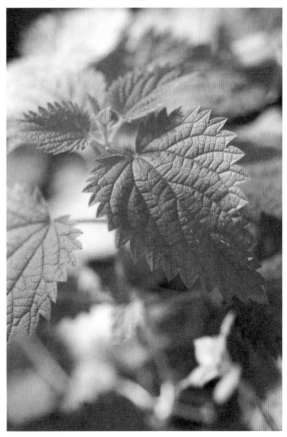

Skin lotions and face packs

Here are some easy recipes for my favorite beautifying skin lotions and face packs.

Marshmallow hand lotion

This is a wonderful lotion for dry, chapped hands.

½ cup (28g) marshmallow root
cold spring water
2 tablespoons ground almonds
1 teaspoon milk
1 teaspoon cider vinegar
lavender oil or olive oil

Chop the marshmallow root finely and soak in cold spring water for 24 hours. Stir and strain well through a cheesecloth-lined sieve. Add one tablespoon of the marshmallow juice to the ground almonds, milk, and cider vinegar. Mix together with a few drops of lavender oil if you want a scented lotion; olive oil if you do not. Pour into a clean, dry, screw-top jar and keep in the fridge, using as required.

Chervil skin cleanser

This is a wonderful cleanser for keeping your skin supple and preventing wrinkles. Infuse a handful of fresh chervil leaves in boiling water and cool, then use the chervil water to cleanse the skin.

Honey and fennel face pack

A sticky face pack made with fennel and honey is said to prevent wrinkles. Chop a bulb of fennel, including the leaves, very finely. Mix with two tablespoons of solid honey, and apply. Leave for 15–20 minutes, then wash off.

Tired eyes

To cool your eyes, make eye pads using thick slices of cucumber. Another option is to use cotton pads soaked in cold milk. Lie down, place the pads on closed eyes and relax for a while.

Borage facial

For a monthly deep facial clean, pour boiling water over a handful of borage leaves in a large bowl. Make a tent with a towel draped over your head and, keeping your eyes tightly closed, steam your face for 10 minutes. If it's too much for you, come up for air when necessary. Rinse your face with cool chervil water.

Strawberry face pack

The juice and flesh of fresh strawberries make a lovely face pack, and are said to whiten skin and lighten freckles. Mash the fruit and spread all over the face—lying down so that it doesn't slide off. After 20 minutes wash off the face pack—or eat it!

BELOW: *If you can resist eating them, strawberries make a great face pack.*

Epsom salts

Epsom salts were much used by our parents' generation in the garden (see pages 105–106). However, they have many beauty uses, too. They contain magnesium sulfate, which is absorbed through the skin when added to bathwater. This draws toxins from the body, soothes the nervous system, reduces swelling, relaxes tired muscles, is a natural emollient, and is also an excellent exfoliator.

Note: It is important to check with your doctor before using Epsom salts if you have any health concerns.

Bath soak

Add 2 cups of Epsom salts to your bathwater for a relaxing and sleep-inducing bath.

Face cleanser

To clean your face at night, mix half a teaspoon of Epsom salts with your regular cleansing cream. Massage into the skin and rinse with cold water.

Skin exfoliator

Massage handfuls of Epsom salts over wet skin in the shower, starting with your feet and continuing up toward the face. Rinse off in warm water.

Foot soak

To soothe aches, remove odors, and soften rough skin, add half a cup of Epsom salts to a large bowl of warm water. Soak your feet for as long as you like, then rinse in warm water and dry thoroughly.

Sprains and bruises

Epsom salts will reduce the swelling caused by sprains and bruises. Add 2 cups to a warm bath and soak.

Removing finger splinters

Soaking the finger in a solution of Epsom salts will draw the splinter out.

AGE SPOT TREATMENT

To delay the appearance of age spots on your hands, or to lighten existing ones, rub a piece of lemon all over your hands before washing. You can also treat freckles in the same way.

CHAPTER 6

INSPIRED GIFTS

During a visit to an outdoor antiques fair, it occurred to me that the atmosphere and bustle were so much more invigorating and pleasing than a crowded department store at Christmas time. Even though the likelihood of losing a possible purchase is far higher than it would be in a crowded shopping mall, the whole ritual of seeking and discovering extraordinary and unexpected treasures is pure pleasure. Could it be because the whole point about antiques is that they are recycled? Most are rare, some are unique, quite a lot are simply garbage, but interesting garbage—somebody once loved each and every object. This is probably the third or fourth time these objects have changed hands. They have all been pre-owned and pre-loved, and here they are again.

Antiques fairs

How likely is it that in 50 years' time the antiques markets of the day will be filled with game boys, plastic toys and flat-screened televisions? I don't think we will marvel at how beautifully these things were made. How terrific would it be if, for just one season, everybody spent the time seeking out vintage gifts rather than new ones? Think of all the energy, pollution, and air miles that could be saved. Not only that, but antiques are usually more beautifully made, could hold their value, or even become more valuable, over the years, and they are more likely to be unique.

As with most advice in this book, this involves more time. However, the time it takes to seek out antiques fairs and find the perfect gift is, in my experience, worth the effort. Start assembling Christmas and birthday presents in January and you might just be able to complete your list by November. What a pleasure to know that you will not have to fight the hysterical crowds in the big stores and spend far more than you intended because you slid into panic-purchase mode.

Lasting enjoyment

This chapter on vintage/recycled/antique artifacts naturally encompasses finding original gifts, but I need no encouragement to furnish my home with antiques—it always has been and always will be a great pleasure. Apart from the obvious joy of buying antiquities, the fact that they have lasted many years and are still earning their keep generations later means that they were worth making in the first place. The sad fact behind our ever-increasing landfill sites is that the time, effort, design, manufacture, and distribution of so much is disregarded so very easily.

A quote by Edmond de Goncourt, an eminent French collector, in an old book written by Barbara Milo Ohrbach, sums up the rules: "If you ever take up collecting, each time you are tempted by a work of art, or by a curio, be sure to ask yourself before deciding to buy: can I live with it,

RIGHT: *An assortment of other people's cast-offs becomes exciting and enticing treasure in the atmosphere of an antiques market. The amazingly wide range of artifacts and curios ensures that there will be something for almost everyone.*

keep it in front of my eyes, and love it until I die?" We might feel this way for approximately one minute about a mass-produced dress, but do we really want to keep it in front of our eyes until we die—I don't think so. However, the tiny lambs (see right) would be very welcome to sit before my eyes until I die—they would be a great pleasure.

The most important thing to remember when buying secondhand goods —because that is what antiquities are—is to love them, not for their potential value, nor for their great practicality, nor because they are fashionable and of the moment, but heed Edmond's wisdom: be sure you will love them until you die. If you are buying for someone else, eccentric, appropriate, amusing, useful, and relevant are all words to which you should add a question mark. If any or all of those words apply, then buy.

Finding inspiration

Antiques have a gentleness not common in our age, and there is often great beauty in the most ordinary of old objects. You may find yourself inspired—and inspire others—to start unusual and fascinating collections. Sellers often specialize in one particular type of item, and have the knack of arranging their wares in an enticing display. The keys photographed here could inspire a whole wall display at little cost. Bowls and baskets of old balls of twine are not only useful but beautiful as well. After getting over the initial shock of receiving a bundle of vintage buttons, I feel sure that, on a dreary winter's afternoon, even a sullen teenager might be moved by the subtle beauty of the buttons and sew them onto an old jacket. They would offer a touch of originality that, in this age of mass marketing, is increasingly difficult to come by.

ABOVE: *An eclectic selection of antique finds.*

BELOW LEFT: *Keys cleverly displayed can make a work of art.*

BELOW: *Button cards are always useful when renovating clothes.*

Paintings and picture frames

You will often find old paintings for sale, many of them by keen amateurs and some of them very fine. It takes time to trawl through the stands but it could prove a rewarding exercise—everybody has room for one more painting and should you be clever enough to find one the subject of which is relevant to the recipient, all the better. If you can't find a suitable painting, look at the multitude of frames for sale and paint or make your own picture.

Antique books

Old, leather-bound books are intriguing and the more random the subject, the better. I am usually initially drawn to beautiful binding, and the contents are secondary. However, old books on, for example, country walks or even midwifery can not only be informative but often hilarious—how to skin and cook a rabbit might well be handy if predictions for our future turn out to be accurate! Gardening books never lose their practicality, and are often filled with good advice long forgotten since pesticides and noxious chemicals took the place of tried-and-tested natural remedies and fertilizers.

China

Saucers that long ago parted company with their cups make lovely soap dishes or (dare I say it) ashtrays. A mishmash of unmatched cups looks great hanging on a dresser. Decorated plates are perfectly acceptable if they are not of a matching set, and could form the start of a collection. Pitchers—small, large, plain, patterned—are lovely planted with a single hyacinth bulb, or snowdrops about to burst into flower. One of these wrapped with gauze makes a fine gift, as does a beautiful cup and saucer filled with homemade, or purchased, confections or bath preparations.

ABOVE: *A cup and saucer, filled with confectionary, makes a thoughtful present.*

BELOW LEFT: *A collection of paintings for sale is always worth looking through.*

BELOW: *Books add warmth to a room and wisdom to a brain.*

Presents for men

Men, whom I find particularly difficult to buy for, are perhaps easier to cater for at antiques fairs. For example, it might be regarded as an insult to give a gift of a new walking stick bought from a store to any man of any age. However, an old, beautifully carved, well-loved walking stick is always a pleasure to carry. If you give a man a plastic measuring tape, I can't help but feel he might be a little disappointed. Yet one of those hand-crafted leather and brass tape measures could become a treasured possession, even though he may never use it for the purpose for which it was originally intended.

The following list gives some ideas for antique gifts for the most challenging people to buy gifts for—men and teenagers—along with their less inspiring present-day alternatives.

Antique gift ideas for men

▸ Leather and brass measuring tape (present-day alternative: plastic and steel measuring tape)

▸ Old leather collar boxes (present-day alternative: a set of plastic storage boxes)

▸ Hand-carved walking stick (present-day alternative: a lightweight aluminum crutch)

▸ A perfect secondhand tweed hacking jacket (present-day alternative: a designer jacket—an unlikely gift)

▸ An old wicker picnic basket (present-day alternative: a new wicker picnic basket—why buy new when there are so many already made?)

▸ Silver flask (present-day alternative: ditto)

▸ Books (present-day alternative: any books of any age are always a delicious gift)

▸ Painting (present-day alternative: anything of any merit is certainly way beyond my budget)

▸ Beautifully crafted garden tools (present-day alternative: I would be happy with anything to do with the garden but old tools have a pleasing feel)

▸ Old glass cloches (present-day alternative: new glass or plastic cloches)

▸ Clocks (present-day alternative: not so pleasing)

▸ Pocket watch (present-day alternative: there isn't one)

▸ Armchair (present-day alternative: a strange or unique gift)

▸ Desk light (present-day alternative: a sad gift)

▸ Glass decanter (present-day alternative: shiny, lumpy, and new—not quite the same)

▸ A set of old terra cotta pots (present-day alternative: shiny and new and frostproof—I wouldn't be pleased)

▸ Enamel compost bucket or two (present-day alternative: a pair of plastic buckets)

▸ A collection of beautiful, wooden-handled corkscrews (present-day alternative: a metal corkscrew)

▸ A lovely bundle of antique silver forks tied with twine (present-day alternative: a posh canteen of silver cutlery)

▸ A collection of different types of twine presented in an old wooden bowl (present-day alternative: a ball of twine)

Antique gift ideas for teenagers

- An old cocktail glass or two (present-day alternative: a set of beer glasses—not good to encourage heavy drinking)
- An interesting painting relevant in some way to the recipient (present-day alternative: a poster)
- A handmade, pure white, lace-trimmed, floor-length Victorian nightdress (present-day alternative: pyjamas)
- An oldfashioned (in good condition) board game—encourages social interaction (present-day alternative: playstation—encourages a solitary life)
- A beautiful old compass in a leather pouch (present-day alternative: a local map)
- A beautifully leather-bound book—relevant in some way to the recipient (present-day alternative: a new book—but isn't the old version more unusual and intriguing?)

FAR LEFT: *Spools of twine make a rather novel arrangement, and nobody can have too much!*

BELOW LEFT: *An old walking stick makes a surprisingly handsome gift for men of all ages.*

BELOW: *Silver cutlery can be bought at antiques fairs for a fraction of the price of new.*

making candles

There's no need to throw away partially burned candles, or to leave them to gather dust in the belief that they somehow look ornamental. It's easy to make new candles, beautiful enough to give away as gifts, by combining the remnants in a decorative container, even reusing an original one.

you will need

Several partially burned candles
Old pan or dish
Decorative container
Sturdy, smooth twine
Long pencil
Scissors

1 Heat the candle remnants in an old pan or dish, either by placing it in a microwave for 1–2 minutes, or in a double saucepan on top of the stove. Be very careful not to burn yourself, either on the pan or with the resulting hot wax. The candles can be heated separately or together, depending on their colors and how many there are.

2 When all the wax is melted, remove any wicks that may remain and pour the wax into your chosen receptacle.

3 Cut a length of sturdy smooth string and tie one end to a pencil, which should be longer than the circumference of the container. Make several knots in the other end of the string to weight it down.

4 Push the knotted end of the string into the wax with the pencil, and then lay the pencil across the receptacle. Move to a cool place to set.

5 When the wax has set hard, cut the string, leaving enough exposed to make a wick.

Caring for antiques

There are a few dos and don'ts for keeping antique items looking as beautiful—or perhaps even more so—as when you bought them.

Antique textiles

Old textiles are extraordinary. The fact that something as simple as a plain linen sheet, woven by hand on a loom and stitched together to cover a mattress, may still be changing hands today for a great deal of money is worthy of contemplation.

Cotton and linen

Luckily, cotton and linen are robust and sturdy fabrics, and respond well to washing. Most cotton and linen pieces can be gently hand washed, or washed in the machine on a gentle cycle. Never use hot water to wash delicate items. You must also never use chlorine bleach on antique fabrics. Lemon juice will do just as good a job, but remember to rinse the fabric in warm water as soon as you have dissolved any stain. Consult the many remedies in Chapter 1 for stained fabrics that can be washed.

Silk and embroidered fabrics

Intricately embroidered pieces or fine silks might need expert advice before cleaning. Try to avoid dry cleaning—unless expressly advised—as the chemicals used may well do more harm than good. Steaming is a good and gentle alternative, although it is still worth taking advice before proceeding.

Storing textiles

Never store textiles in dry, hot attics, nor damp cellars. Ideally, the temperature should be kept constant and humidity at around 55 percent.

Antique clothes

Do not store antique clothes on a hanger; instead, lie them flat. If possible, roll rather than fold them as the fabric weakens along the folds. If a large item, such as a quilt, has to be folded, lay acidfree tissue paper along the line of the fold to prevent deep creasing. Once or twice a year, refold the item to prevent permanent lines from forming.

Preventing textiles from fading

Keep precious textiles, including framed needlework, vintage cushions, antique quilts

BELOW: *Old French linen is now rare, and the fewer items available, the more expensive they become.*

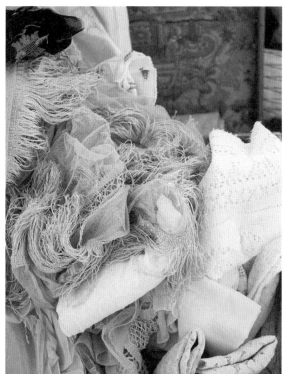

and rugs, out of strong sunlight. If you have a large and precious rug that, of necessity, has to be left left in strong light, turn the rug regularly so that the natural fading will be equal on both sides.

Drying in sunlight
The sun will bleach robust white fabrics beautifully. Do not dry delicate items in the sun because this will contribute to their demise. Never dry precious, colored, washable items in the sun, as they will fade. Sometimes this is desirable: there is many a time I have transformed a garishly colored item into a beautiful, faded antique with the help of the sun and some lemon juice.

Drying delicate items
Never hang delicate items to dry; always lay them flat on a cotton towel. Otherwise the weight of the water combined with gravity could well rip the fabric, especially if it is lace.

Machine washing lace
If you have a fairly robust item decorated with fine lace, place it in a net bag or pillowcase before putting in the washing machine and washing on a gentle cycle.

Rug and carpet care
Keep precious rugs clean with regular vacuuming. If you feel they need washing, find an expert rug cleaner. If you are having difficulty finding someone, ask in a store that specializes in rugs as they may well know of a reputable cleaner.

Many rugs woven in Afghanistan, India, or Africa are most probably much more robust than you imagine. In order to give their handicraft a more lived-in, aged patina, makers often lay carpets in the road for cars to drive over—they come to little harm and just get more beautiful. Remember this when you find yourself delicately dabbing at a stain.

Silver
Browsing in antiques markets can often yield great silver purchases. Complete sets of silver cutlery are usually more expensive than when sold loose, so consider buying single pieces.

Hand washing
Be very careful when washing metal pieces that have a baize or felt covering on the base, such as silver candlesticks and wine coasters. Do not immerse in water. Wash upside down or wipe with a damp cloth.

Wax drippings
To remove wax drippings from an intricate candlestick, turn it upside down and, holding it over a piece of old newspaper, blow hot air from a hairdryer to melt the wax. Don't throw away the newspaper. Instead, fold into a long strip lengthways and tie into a knot—you can then use it to light fires.

Wooden handles
If you are cleaning an item with a wooden handle, such as a silver teapot or coffee pot, polish the handle with beeswax before cleaning the silver part. This will protect the wood from damage by water.

Dusting silver
Keep silver dusted with a soft paint brush. If you dust with a cloth, you are more likely to scratch the surface.

Storing silver
When storing silver, keep a large piece of chalk in the drawer with it to prevent tarnishing.

Washing in a dishwasher
You can wash silver cutlery in the dishwasher but never with other metals such as aluminum or stainless steel. If you do, the silver will tarnish unnecessarily.

rosebud potpourri

Scented herbs and flowers, often complemented by a variety of spices, have been used since Roman times to perfume rooms, repel insects such as ants, and ward off germs. Nowadays, potpourri is often used ornamentally, displayed in a variety of decorative dishes and containers. Any herbs, flower buds or petals can be used, but sometimes it's nice to concentrate on just one flower, such as these pretty rosebuds.

you will need

Rosebuds

Newspaper

Orange

Lemon or lime

Vegetable peeler

China bowl

Cinnamon sticks, cardamom pods
or whole nutmegs (optional)

1 Collect as many rosebuds as you can through the spring and summer and spread them out on newspaper or in trays to dry, preferably in the sun.

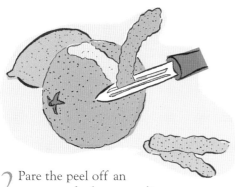

2 Pare the peel off an orange and a lemon or lime. Cut into strips and lay them out to dry with the rosebuds.

3 Meanwhile, find a china bowl that you would like to display— buy one from an antiques fair or secondhand store if necessary. When the rosebuds and the peel are completely dry, mix them all together in the bowl with your hands. If you want a spicier aroma, add some cinnamon sticks or cardamom pods, or whole nutmegs.

covering a book with vintage fabric

Many treasures are to be found in secondhand bookstores or on the bookstalls of antiques fairs. An old book on a relevant subject makes a thoughtful and unusual present. Covering it in a scrap of vintage fabric makes it unique.

you will need
Vintage fabric
Scissors
Hardback book
Fabric adhesive

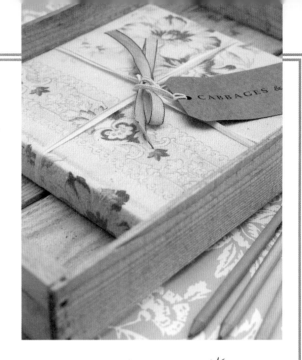

1 Cut out the fabric to the size of the book plus an extra 1 in. (2.5cm) all around. Open the book, lay it face down, and cover the outside with fabric adhesive. Turn it over and position it carefully on the fabric, allowing the 1 in. (2.5cm) border all around.

2 If the book has a wide spine, cut the fabric on each side up to the spine, top and bottom. Cut off the resulting flap of fabric, leaving a small amount to tuck in down the spine.

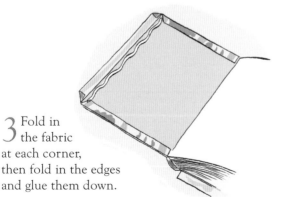

3 Fold in the fabric at each corner, then fold in the edges and glue them down.

4 Glue the first page onto the cover to hide the glued edges.

Glass

Antique glassware is often especially beautiful but its fragility demands special care.

Washing

When washing fine antique glasses, never put them into the sink together. Line the sink with a dish towel to make a padded base. Fill with lukewarm water and add a cupful of vinegar. Wash them one at a time very carefully—old glass is often finer then modern glass and will easily chip or crack. Do not use very hot water because this can crack fine glass.

Drying

Air dry glass by placing it upside down on a flat surface on a clean, dry dish towel.

Cloudy glass

If you have problems with cloudy glass—also known as "sick" glass—try soaking it in vinegar. Sometimes, however, this bloom found in old glass is permanent. If the item is particularly precious to you, you could seek the advice of an expert.

Decanters

See page 30 for hints on cleaning the hard-to-reach insides of glass decanters.

> **CAUTION**
> *Never put old, fine glass in the dishwasher—it is always best washed by hand.*

Wood

There is real joy in looking after old wood to bring out its natural beauty.

Waxing wood

Never over-wax wooden objects. A thin layer of beeswax three or four times a year is ample. Polish off the wax with a soft cloth following the grain of the wood. Building up many fine layers of wax is the way to achieve a deep patina. Too much wax is difficult to remove and attracts dust.

Dusting ornate wood

Keep wooden objects free from dust, using a soft brush to remove dust on intricate carved pieces, including picture frames.

LEFT: *Antique glass decanters in good condition are often more beautiful than new versions.*

Paper

Storing prints and documents

Handle old prints and documents with great care, if you need to handle them at all. To store, separate them with sheets of acidfree tissue paper.

Dusting books

Keep old books free of dust as much as possible using a soft brush especially for this purpose. With the book closed, flick the dust away from the binding. Always remove books from their shelves before dusting.

Precious prints

When framing precious prints, make sure that the framer inserts acidfree backing paper to preserve the print. If you buy a framed print of particular importance, it is worth taking it to a framer to insert acidfree paper even if the frame seems perfect.

Display prints

Strong sunlight damages and fades paper and artwork. If possible, display framed prints out of sunlight.

Remove staples

Always remove staples from paper—if left in, they will cause rust marks.

Ceramics

Washing

Use a small amount of detergent or white distilled vinegar in lukewarm water.

Mended china

Never submerge mended pieces of china in water because this will weaken the adhesive.

RIGHT AND FAR RIGHT: *A random collection of china on a market stall. Try to buy pieces that are uncracked if they are to be used for serving food or drink.*

Drying

As with glass, always dry items by lying them carefully on a folded dish towel.

Removing stains

To remove stains from within a china or ceramic cup, soak with a solution of white distilled vinegar, adding some baking soda (bicarbonate of soda) for difficult stains.

Dusting ornate pieces

For dusting intricate pieces, use a medium soft watercolor paint brush to get into the little crevices.

Finally ...

If you have read this book from cover to cover, I hope it will have made an impact on the way you live day to day. If ecological issues become so much part of all our lives, we will begin to take for granted that lights are never left burning unnecessarily; that we never throw things away that can be recycled or re-used; that we never leave water running unnecessarily.

If we refuse to accept plastic bags and excessive packaging, then without noticing we will be making a huge difference. If, as a matter of course, we order bulky nonperishable items via the internet once every three months, then our shopping can be done in an old-fashioned way—on foot with a shopping basket. If we are buying produce seasonally, with as few intermediaries as possible between source and purchase, we can have an idea of how our food is produced.

If we just stop, take stock of the way we live and do 12 of the things listed below every day for the rest of our lives, then we will make a difference. If we can delay global warming for long enough to work out a plan to reverse it, then we can, together, feel less ashamed when we hand our beautiful planet over to the next generation.

- Switch off all unnecessary lights
- Switch off all appliances with a standby light
- Shower for one minute less every day
- Use gray water to water the garden and wash the car
- Boil only enough water to fill your immediate needs
- Grow three herbs
- Grow ten flowers
- Walk instead of using the car once a week
- Take a vacation at home now and then
- Plant grass instead of installing decking
- Recycle all your paper
- Only use recycled toilet tissue

- Try using the cleaning products listed in this book for one whole month
- Make sure every present you give this year has been enjoyed by someone before
- Buy a water filter and buy bottled water only in an extreme emergency
- Place a bottle filled with water or a brick in your toilet cistern
- When you buy your next car, make it as environmentally efficient as you can bear
- Ask stores why they are heating the pavement
- Ask stores why they keep their lights on through the night
- Ask stores if it is necessary to have automatically opening doors that are activated by people walking by and not by people walking in
- Choose ten products per week made or grown by organic methods
- Read labels—not for a product's calorific content, but for its green credentials
- Read labels and try where you can to buy produce made in your own country
- Buy local
- Buy seasonal
- Cook from scratch using what you have grown
- Store what you have grown
- Switch your computer and printer off when you stop using it
- Print only those things that are absolutely necessary
- Turn your heating down, and wear more clothes
- Buy an ordinary old-fashioned handheld fan, so for an hour or two a day you can switch off the air conditioning
- Take the train instead of an aeroplane
- Take a bicycle instead of the car
- Walk to your destination once a week
- Learn to respect the planet
- Teach your children to respect the planet

useful contacts

Energy

www.eere.energy.gov/greenpower
This U. S. government site, Energy Efficiency and Renewable Energy, gives advice on finding a green energy supplier.

www.ases.org
The American Solar Energy Society provides information on solar energy for homes and businesses.

Home and Garden

Cabbages & Roses
www.cabbagesandroses.com
A family-owned fashion, fabric, and accessories company committed to ethical production. Made as much as possible with www.oeko-tex.com standards, in limited quantities, in the UK.

Colour Makes People Happy
www.makespeoplehappy.co.uk
An entirely natural, eco-friendly paint company. The paint is made with local ingredients from the South Downs.

Dalefoot Composts
www.dalefootcomposts.co.uk
Suppliers of peat-free and bracken-based compost.

Edward Bulmer Natural Paints
www.edwardbulmerpaint.co.uk
Non-toxic natural paints made from raw materials such as plant extracts, chalk, earth minerals and linseed. Most have full organic or equivalent certification.

Good Energy
www.goodenergy.co.uk
A British company supplying only 100% renewable energy.

Greenshop
www.greenshop.co.uk
Sustainable, eco-friendly products for the home.

Little Greene Paint & Paper
www.littlegreene.com
Odorless, water-based paints with the industry's lowest eco-rating and with virtually zero Volatile organic compounds (VOCs).

www.eco-age.com
Fulfils all ecologically sound needs in the home.

Beauty and Fashion

AS Apothecary
www.asapoth.com
A small-batch distillery making natural scents, creams, aromatic waters, and balms from flowers, bark, leaves, roots, blossom, and moss that they grow or forage in the fields, mountains, and gardens of Sussex, Cyprus, and Scotland.

Beyond Skin
www.beyond-skin.com
Ethically-made vegan footwear.

Depop
www.depop.com
Buy and sell fashion online.

Mashu
www.mashu.co.uk
A handbag and accessories company using premium sustainable and recycled materials.

Slack Shoemakers
www.slackshoemakers.com
Shoemakers who work with ecologically tanned leather. Sole shanks using recyclable wood chip. Shoes really made to last.

Vestiaire Collective
www.vestiairecollective.com
Platform for selling unwanted designer clothes and accessories.

Flowers

Aesme Flower Studio & Garden
www.aesme.co.uk
Ethically- and sustainably-grown flowers.

The Real Flower Company
www.realflowers.co.uk
Ethically-grown and fair-trade flowers.

Food

http://afsic.nal.usda.gov
The Alternative Farming Systems Information Center, a Department of Agriculture body, offers a wealth of information on sustainable food systems and a list of Web sites for Community Supported Agriculture throughout the U. S.

www.ams.usda.gov/farmersmarkets/map.htm
How to find farmers' markets in your state.

www.wholefoodsmarkets.com
This leading retailer of natural and organic foods has more than 265 stores in North America and Britain.

Riverford Organic Farmers
www.riverford.co.uk
Organic fruit and vegetables from a cooperatively run farm.

General

Ebay
www.ebay.com
Platform for selling anything and everything.

Real Simple
www.realsimple.com
A treasure trove of good-to-know information with inspiring ideas for the home.

Soil Association
www.soilassociation.org
An independent nonprofit that sets organic standards and supports and offers advice to organic farmers.

Sustainable Food Trust
www.sustainablefoodtrust.org
Working to accelerate the transition to more sustainable food and farming systems, to the health of both humans and the planet.

index

acknowledgments

Thank you to my publishers Cico Books, especially Cindy Richards who had enough confidence in me to ask me to write this book, and Gillian Haslam and Marion Paull for their help in editing. To Lucinda Symons and her assistant Francesca Day who spent many days making beautiful photographs, and to Christine Wood for making it all coherent and even more beautiful.

To Chris and Lucy Rich for their exquisite farm and shop providing inspiration for all, and Emmeline Johnston for allowing us to photograph her perfect allotment. To all at Cabbages & Roses, especially Linda Cardona, Amy Gibbons and Kate Strutt, and to my family Mark and Edward Strutt for letting me write in the kitchen. To John and Jack Robinson for cabbages and black currant juice.

And to all those who are making us aware of our beautiful, beautiful planet and are working towards solutions to save it.

www.louissachar.co.uk